EXECUTIONS

700 YEARS OF PUBLIC PUNISHMENT IN LONDON

JACKIE KEILY, THOMAS ARDILL,
BEVERLEY COOK & MERIEL JEATER

EXECUTIONS

700 YEARS
of PUBLIC
PUNISHMENT
IN LONDON

 PWP

Philip Wilson Publishers
Bloomsbury Publishing Plc
50 Bedford Square, London, WC1B 3DP, UK
29 Earlsfort Terrace, Dublin 2, Ireland

Bloomsbury, Philip Wilson Publishers and the Philip Wilson
logo are trademarks of Bloomsbury Publishing Plc

Published on the occasion of the exhibition: *Executions,*
Museum of London, 14 October 2022–16 April 2023

First published in Great Britain in 2022
Copyright © Museum of London, 2022

Jackie Keily, Thomas Ardill, Beverley Cook and Meriel Jeater
have asserted their rights under the Copyright, Designs and
Patents Act, 1988, to be identified as Authors of this work

A catalogue record for this book is available from the
British Library

Library of Congress Cataloguing-in-Publication
data has been applied for

ISBN: 978-1-78130-108-1

2 4 6 8 10 9 7 5 3 1

Designed and typeset by Ocky Murray
Printed and bound in the UK by Gomer Press

MIX
Paper from
responsible sources
FSC® C114687
www.fsc.org

To find out more about our authors and books visit
www.bloomsbury.com and sign up for our newsletters

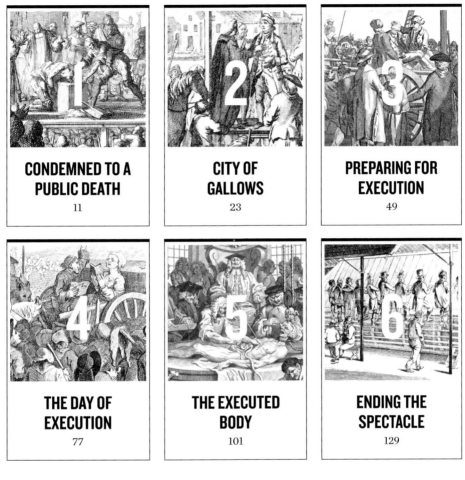

CONTENTS

INTRODUCTION

Imagine the roar of the crowd, the push and pull as hundreds, even thousands, of people surge forwards to get a better view. How large, uncontrolled groups behave today may not be so dissimilar to the actions of those attending public executions in the past. Or picture a Punch and Judy show, a feature of London's street entertainment since the 1660s and traditionally a tale of domestic violence: Mr Punch beats his baby and is chased by a parish constable, the Beadle, and the Hangman, who is named after the notorious 17th-century London executioner, Jack Ketch. A show aimed at children, wrapped up in brightly coloured costumes, yet featuring a gallows and a very public execution. As with the Punch and Judy show, most people who attended, or even read about, a public execution in London did so safe in the knowledge that it was something that would never touch their lives – or at least they hoped so.

Tens of thousands of people were publicly executed in London between the first recorded execution at Tyburn in 1196 and the end of public execution in Britain in 1868. Over that time, hundreds of thousands of Londoners and visitors queued to watch these spectacles, bought food and drink, craned their necks to see what was happening and then returned home, perhaps to sleep peacefully, comforted by the just fulfilment of the law, or to be wracked by nightmares of the hangman's noose. Today, the idea of people thronging into central London to watch someone being executed seems bizarre. It is perhaps hard to understand or identify with such an extreme fascination, but it needs to be viewed in the context of a time when pain, suffering and death were more visible, and often played out on London's streets as an acceptable part of urban life. Executions took place in public to show people what happened to those who broke the law. For hundreds of years, the authorities relied on the spectacle to deter crime and rebellion and to demonstrate the ultimate power of the Crown, Church and state over the life and death of its citizens. By the end of the 18th century, there were over 200 capital offences, from murder and treason to sodomy and theft, forming a harsh penal system known as the 'Bloody Code' (see page 140). The nature of the crime was reflected in the method of execution: the most horrific deaths were reserved for traitors, while the majority of common criminals were hanged. The executed body was often publicly displayed as a deterrent, or 'destroyed' through dissection or dismemberment. As both the capital city and the most populous place in Britain, London's courts condemned more people to death than any other city. By the 18th century, hanging days were viewed as public holidays and took place, on average, eight times a year, corresponding to the eight Old Bailey Sessions, the criminal trials for the City of London and the County of Middlesex.

It would be naïve, however, to view our ancestors' interest in attending or reading about public execution as purely about moral instruction or deterrence. Fascination with sudden violent death and its consequences has always been a part of the human condition. There was a strong performative aspect to public executions themselves: from the preparations for execution, with set routines and traditions, to the very public journey to the place of execution, and the stage-like scaffold. Those about to be executed were at the centre of the audience's attention. Some of the condemned carefully chose their clothing for the day of execution, others prepared speeches or prayers. Certain criminals became celebrities, some famous, others infamous – the thief and serial

↓ *An illustration of an open-air Punch and Judy show.*
FROM LONDON: A PILGRIMAGE, BY BLANCHARD JERROLD AND GUSTAVE DORÉ, 1872.

escapee John 'Jack' Sheppard (1702–24) achieved an almost mythical fame and heroic status among London's working class. By the 18th century, portraits of the most famous were being commissioned, while cheaper engravings and broadsides became souvenirs to be collected by the inquisitive public. These increased in popularity in the 19th century, along with newspaper reports. The latter ensured that the intimate details of the investigation and trial, as well as the execution, became widespread public knowledge, syndicated across the country and the wider world.

But as the 19th century progressed, in parallel with this fascination, attitudes were changing. Public pain and suffering were becoming increasingly unacceptable to a Victorian society that valued privacy, and discouraged visible displays of the darker side of life. A new moral code was emerging, witnessed by penal and social reforms, that sat uneasily alongside a system of state punishment played out on crowded streets. The long history of public execution in London was coming to an end.

Tyburn, Newgate and Tower Hill are all famous public execution sites in London, but there were once many more; and for all the infamous criminals who were executed, far more have been forgotten. The history of execution on London's streets is a disturbing one, but it is also one that impacted real people and real lives. This is a story of those condemned to a public death in London, the crowds that watched them perish, and the impact of executions on the capital's landscape and society.

← ↑ Puppets of Punch, Judy, the Beadle, the Hangman and the gallows, c.1830. Public executions took place sometimes on a daily basis on London's street corners and markets, in the form of Punch and Judy shows. These puppets and model gallows date to the 1830s or earlier.

CHAPTER I

The death penalty / Drawing, hanging and quartering /
Beheading / Boiling / Burning / Hanging

CONDEMNED TO A PUBLIC DEATH

Public execution likely took place in London in the Roman period and in the centuries after, but it is only from the 12th century onwards that records of public execution in London exist. The crimes a person could be executed for and how people were executed varied through time. By the 18th century, hanging was by far the most common method used. The last person to be publicly executed in London was Michael Barrett, in 1868. Execution as a form of punishment, however, continued away from public view until 1964.

The earliest record of a public execution taking place in London is from 1196 at Tyburn. Located to the west of the City of London, it was to be the main place of execution for the city until the late 18th century. A contemporary chronicler, Ralph Diceto, describes William FitzOsbert, who had rebelled against the king, being dragged behind a horse from the City of London to Tyburn where he was hanged, along with a number of his supporters. The fact that he was taken to Tyburn indicates it was already a site of execution. What is not known is when it began to be used as such.

THE DEATH PENALTY

It was during the 12th century, under King Henry II, that England's common law began to be codified and uniformly enforced. The Treason Act of 1351 distinguished between high treason (crimes against the monarch) and petty treason (murder of one's superior, which at that time included a wife's murder of her husband or a servant their employer). The penalty for the former was to be drawn, hanged and quartered for a man, or drawn and burned for a woman. For petty treason the penalty was slightly lessened, to being drawn and hanged for a man, or burned for a woman. Other crimes such as arson, heresy, counterfeiting and murder were also capital crimes. During the 18th century, the number of offences that were punishable by a mandatory death sentence increased from about 50 in 1688 to over 200 by the end of the 1700s: what later became known as the period of the 'Bloody Code' (see page 140). It was brought to an end by the Judgement of Death Act in 1823, which gave judges the discretion to pass a lesser sentence, except in cases of treason or murder. The years of the 1700s through to 1823 therefore saw a peak in the number of people who were condemned to death in London.

↑ *William de Marisco, drawn from the Tower of London to the gallows, 1242.* This illustration by Matthew Paris, in his manuscript *Chronica Majora*, shows the 'traitor William de Marisco drawn to the gallows'. De Marisco had conspired to assassinate King Henry III. He was sentenced to be drawn, hanged and quartered with sixteen of his followers, and the execution probably took place at Tyburn.

DRAWING, HANGING AND QUARTERING

Dating back to the 12th century, drawing, hanging and quartering was an ancient punishment for treason. Traitors were 'drawn', which involved being dragged through the streets by horse to

Execution of
In the Gunpowder

the Conspirators
Plot in the Year 1606.

Published May 1, 1795. by J.Caulfield.

the execution site, hanged until they were nearly dead, then castrated, disembowelled, beheaded and cut into quarters. Originally traitors were dragged along the ground, as shown in the image of William de Marisco, but, as this could kill them before the execution, they were later drawn on wicker or wooden panels, ox hides, or sledges. The multiple excruciating punishments were meant to reflect the seriousness of the crime and not all elements were used in every case. For example, when eight of the conspirators who had plotted to blow up Parliament in November 1605, in what became known as the Gunpowder Plot, were found guilty, they received the full sentence. Each was dragged through the crowded streets of London to their execution site, where they were hanged but cut down while still conscious. They were then castrated, disembowelled and their bodies quartered. On the second day of the executions, 31 January 1606, two of the men, including Guy Fawkes, jumped from the gallows in an effort to

↑ *The Gunpowder Plot conspirators being drawn, hanged and quartered, 30 and 31 January 1606.*

Four were publicly executed in St Paul's Churchyard in the City of London and four, including Guy Fawkes, in Old Palace Yard, Westminster. The setting of this reissued Dutch engraving resembles neither of these sites, and also conflates the two execution days. The details of the punishments, however, are vividly portrayed.

ENGRAVING, AFTER CLAES JANSZ VISSCHER, PUBLISHED BY JAMES CAULFIELD, 1795.

avoid the worst part of the sentence, but only Fawkes succeeded in breaking his neck. His body was disembowelled and quartered. The sentence continued to be used into the 19th century but, by then, traitors were hanged until dead and then decapitated.

BEHEADING

Noble men and women condemned for treason were often beheaded out of respect for their high status, and did not have to suffer the agonising and humiliating alternatives of drawing, hanging and quartering, or burning. From the late 14th century until the mid 18th century, most public beheadings in London took place on Tower Hill, outside the Tower of London. A smaller number occurred in private inside the Tower grounds, including those of King Henry VIII's wives Anne Boleyn and Katherine Howard.

Beheadings were usually undertaken by the official executioner for London, using an axe, but this was not always the case. In 1538, Margaret Pole, Countess of Salisbury, a Catholic and cousin of King Henry VIII, was arrested and charged with treason at the age of 67. Her religion and close relationship to the King placed her in a dangerous position. She spent two and a half years in the Tower before being executed on 27 May 1541 within the Tower precincts. An account of the execution records that the official executioner was not available and so a less experienced youth took his place. Either owing to his nerves and lack of experience or to Margaret's moving unexpectedly, he ended up striking her eleven times before finally decapitating her. When James Scott, the Duke of Monmouth, was beheaded for high treason on Tower Hill by the public executioner, Jack Ketch, the latter botched the execution and is said to have resorted to using a knife. Monmouth was the

↓ Beheading of the Duke of Monmouth, 1685.
Monmouth asked the axeman, Jack Ketch, to finish him in one go. However, after he'd taken five or more blows, and with onlookers horrified by the sight of the duke rising up at least once from the block, Ketch resorted to using a knife.

ENGRAVING BY JAN LUYKEN, PUBLISHED BY JAN CLAESZ TEN HOORN, 1689.

eldest illegitimate son of King Charles II. In 1685, he led a rebellion to seize the throne from his uncle King James II and was condemned to death. When Anne Boleyn was executed for adultery and treason in 1536, it was done, at her request, by an expert swordsman who travelled from Calais especially for the execution.

The Jacobite rebel Simon Fraser, Lord Lovat, was the last person to be beheaded on Tower Hill in 1747, at the age of 80. He was a supporter of Charles Edward Stuart, the Young Pretender, in the rebellion of 1745 against King George II. Lovat was also the final person to be decapitated alive; subsequent traitors were hanged first. No judicial beheadings took place after 1820, although this execution method was only formally abolished in 1973.

BOILING

Death by boiling appears to have been carried out only a handful of times. In February 1531, cook Richard Roose poisoned the porridge for the household of John Fisher, Bishop of Rochester, causing two deaths. King Henry VIII declared this crime to be treason and Parliament passed the 'Acte for Poysoning', ordering murderers who used poison to be boiled to death. Although extremely unusual, it is likely that boiling had been used as a method of execution before this, but it was Roose's crime that led to its entering the statute books. Roose was boiled at Smithfield on 5 April 1531. According to a contemporary chronicle, he was dipped up and down into the boiling water until he was dead. Eleven years later, Margaret Davies (or Davy), a maid, suffered the same fate for poisoning four people in the house she lived in. Henry's son King Edward VI ended this execution method when he became king in 1547.

BURNING

Public execution by burning at the stake has a long history, and was used as punishment for a number of different crimes. It was also used for women as an alternative to other forms of execution. In his *Commentaries on the Laws of England*, published between 1765 and 1770, William Blackstone attributed this difference to the 'decency due to the [female] sex [which] forbids the exposing and mangling their bodies'. In the medieval period, burning to death was sometimes used as a punishment for arson, and, in 1401, an act of Parliament enabled it to be used for those

'But the flame coming to his hand, in the space of a second, he let it go, when she gave three dreadful shrieks, and with her hands and feet beat down the faggots.'

Ipswich Journal, 7 September 1726, describing the death of Catherine Hayes

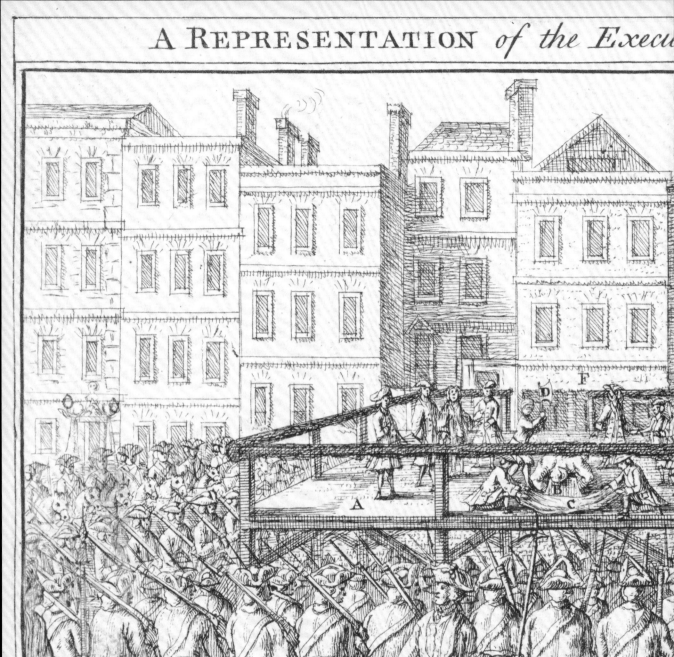

A . *The Scaffold .*
B . *Lord Lovat's head on ŷ Block.*
C . *Cloth to receive the Head .*
D . *The Executioner with ŷ Axe.*
E . *The (*
F . *The (*

on of Lord LOVAT.

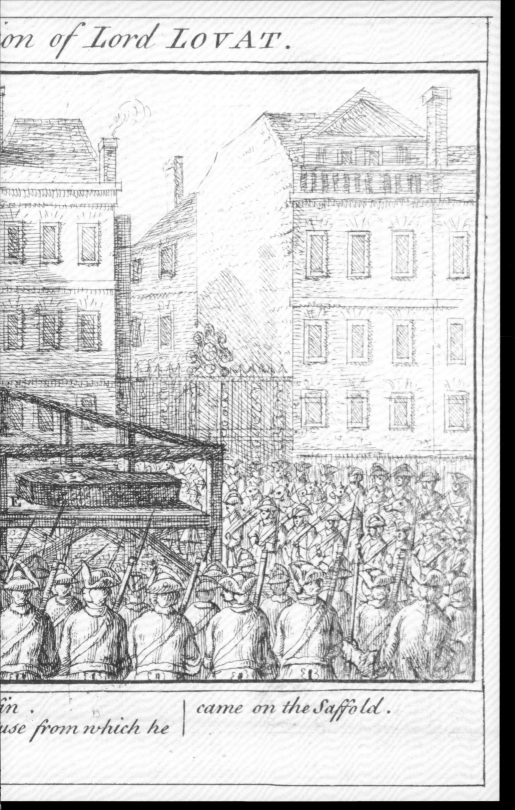

ïn .
use from which he | came on the Saffold .

found guilty of heresy. It aimed to 'strike fear into the minds' of people who questioned the teachings of the Church and, in particular, those who were followers of Lollardy, an early form of Protestantism. In March 1401, William Sawtrey became the first Lollard to be burned at the stake for his beliefs, at Smithfield. This form of punishment became increasingly common during the religious upheavals of the 16th century in England. King Henry VIII's break with the Catholic Church in 1534 introduced a period of Reformation, culminating in the adoption of Protestantism under his son, King Edward VI, and the increased persecution of Catholics. In 1553, Edward died and his sister, Queen Mary I, a Catholic, took power. Mary's reign, although only five years, was a period of Counter-Reformation and saw the persecution of many Protestants. Over 280 religious dissenters were burned at the stake in England, leading to her nickname 'Bloody Mary'. Forty-three of these 'protestant martyrs' died at Smithfield, while others were executed at Stratford-le-Bow, Barnet, Islington, Southwark, Uxbridge, Westminster and elsewhere in England.

↑ *Protestant martyrs burned at the stake in Smithfield, 27 January 1556.*

It was not unusual for a number of heretics to be burned together. Here, seven individuals are shown: Thomas Whittle, priest; Barthelet Greene, gentleman; John Tudson, craftsman; John Went, craftsman; Thomas Browne; Isabelle Foster, wife; Joan Warner alias Latchford, maid. All await their fate as straw or sticks are being stacked up around them, ready to be set alight.

WOODCUT, PUBLISHED IN FOXE'S BOOK OF MARTYRS, 1610.

Engraved for The Malefactor's Register

The manner of BURNING *a* WOMAN *convicted of Treason.*

← *Catherine Hayes being burned at the stake at Tyburn for petty treason, 1726.*

Catherine Hayes, condemned to death for murdering her husband (petty treason), is said to have been the last woman to be burned alive. The executioner was intending to strangle her first, but the fire took hold too early, burning his hands and causing him to drop the rope with which he would have strangled her.

ENGRAVING BY JOHN LODGE AFTER DANIEL DODD, 1776.

Women who had committed coinage crimes, such as counterfeiting, or 'petty treason', such as murdering their husbands, were also sentenced to be burned. In 1656, burning alive for murder was abolished and instead women were strangled first, and then burned. The last woman to be burned in London was Catherine Murphy, also known as Christian Bowman, in 1789. She and her husband were found guilty of counterfeiting and were sentenced to death. Murphy's husband was hanged, but Murphy herself was strangled and then burned, because she was a woman. The practice of burning people was abolished the following year.

HANGING

Hanging was the most common form of execution for the widest range of crimes. Until the end of public execution in 1868, the 'short-drop' method was used, where criminals were hanged from a noose and strangled to death by their own body weight. This agonising death could take several minutes, although people were usually left hanging for an hour to ensure they were dead.

The earliest hangings used a tree or crude wooden gallows from which a rope was suspended. The condemned was supported from below, with their head in the noose. The support – a ladder, horse or, more usually, a cart – was then removed and the person was left suspended. Sometimes family members or the executioner would pull on the legs of the hanged person to speed up their death. The use of a cart can be clearly seen on the playing card depicting the execution of Robert Green, Henry Berry and Lawrence Hill on Primrose Hill in 1679, for the murder of Sir Edmund Berry Godfrey. In the late 17th century, there was a rise in anti-Catholic feeling in England and it reached its climax with the Popish Plot, an alleged Catholic plot against King Charles II. Godfrey, a Protestant politician, was involved in the investigation and when he was found dead, the Catholic Green, Berry and Hill were framed for his murder and executed.

In 1760, a purpose-built platform was introduced with a form of trapdoor upon which the condemned stood; when opened, it left them suspended. This was first used for the execution of Laurence Shirley, 4th Earl Ferrers, at Tyburn. Ferrers had murdered his steward. As a peer, he was tried at Westminster Hall and found guilty of murder. He petitioned to be beheaded at the Tower, since he was an aristocrat, but the Murder Act 1752 only allowed for hanging as the penalty for murder and so, he was hanged as a common criminal at Tyburn. The new trapdoor mechanism was located on a special gallows and dressed in black cloth for the occasion.

↓ *A cart pulling away from the gallows, 11 February 1679.*
This printed playing card depicts the hanging of Robert Green, Henry Berry and Lawrence Hill. It comes from a set published as a means of spreading political propaganda. The men strain against the ropes as the cart pulls away.

ENGRAVED PLAYING CARD BY FRANCIS BARLOW, PUBLISHED 1679.

Under William Marwood, the executioner from 1874 to 1883, the 'long drop' became the standard method of hanging people within prisons. It caused the neck to break and offered a much faster death than strangulation. This was a more scientific method initially developed in Ireland and based on calculating the weight of the prisoner's clothed body; however, it was by no means completely reliable and some still died of strangulation.

CITY OF GALLOWS

If you walk up Newgate Street, navigate the intersection at Marble Arch or pass the junction of Borough High Street and Harper Road, it is hard to imagine that, as the sites of Newgate Prison, Tyburn and the Surrey County Gaol, these locations hosted hundreds of executions, witnessed by thousands of people. Public execution took place all over London, and the capital had several execution sites that were used regularly for centuries. Sometimes executions were held in significant public spaces and, for particularly heinous or high-profile offences, criminals could be executed close to the site of their crime.

It wasn't just the execution that was public. After death, the body, or parts of the body, of the executed, could be displayed to remind the public of what would happen if they broke the law. At sites across the city, the public could encounter the bodily remains of the executed hanging in cages or affixed to the city gates, or traitors' heads on spikes over London Bridge. Gibbets were placed by the main roads into the city and along the River Thames so no one entering the capital could escape witnessing the fatal consequences of crime.

SMITHFIELD

Smithfield, a district north-west of the City of London, was used for various public purposes in the medieval and Tudor periods, including a livestock market, fairs and executions. In 1305, Scottish nobleman Sir William Wallace was found guilty of treason and executed there. The majority of those executed at Smithfield were religious dissenters, particularly during the peak of the Reformation and Counter-Reformation in the 16th century. The burning of heretics at Smithfield was a conspicuous demonstration of the state's intolerance of religious dissent. However, it also created a very public site of martyrdom, as those condemned to execution were allowed a final opportunity to protest their innocence or demonstrate the strength of their faith. Bartholomew Legate, executed at Smithfield in 1612, was the last person to be burned at the stake in London for their religious beliefs. Plaques commemorating Sir William Wallace and the Smithfield Martyrs can be found at St Bartholomew's Hospital.

TYBURN

Tyburn served as London's principal site of execution for around 600 years. The earliest account records the execution of William FitzOsbert in 1196. The infamous Triple Tree or Tyburn Tree, a triangular gallows that allowed for simultaneous multiple hangings, was set up in 1571 and was first depicted in the 1607 version of Norden's Map of Middlesex. Until the late 18th century, Tyburn was a semi-rural location on the north-western outskirts of London, about 4.5 kilometres from Newgate Prison. This meant that most of the condemned had to make a long and very public journey. Located at the junction of two roads (modern-day Edgware Road and Oxford Street, by Marble Arch), Tyburn was easily accessible by foot or coach and, because it was in more open countryside, it could accommodate thousands of

→ *The martyrdom of John Bradford and John Leaf in Smithfield, 1 July 1555.* John Bradford, a Protestant preacher, was burned at Smithfield, during the reign of Queen Mary I, with a 19-year-old apprentice, called John Leaf. Before he was set alight, Bradford told Leaf to 'Be of good comfort brother; for we shall have a merry supper with the Lord this night!'
ETCHING, PUBLISHED BY THOMAS BOWLES II, C.1746–55.

'...they paraded the grisly apparatus of death through almost every quarter of London. There is scarcely a street [...] in which it has not planted its black foot...'
Charles Knight, publisher and author, *London*, 1841

Jesus receive us
Repent England

spectators. Wealthy visitors hired a place in the stands erected and managed by local landowners like Mother Proctor whose 'pew' operated from around 1724. It was alleged that she earned £500, the equivalent of over £50,000 today, at the execution of Earl Ferrers in 1760.

The last executions at Tyburn took place in 1783, by which time the surrounding area was becoming developed and gentrified as London expanded. This gentrification also meant that there was less appetite for the public spectacle of the condemned's journey from the City of London to Tyburn and for the disruption it caused to the flow, stability and economy of the city.

→ *Map of Middlesex with Tyburn's 'Triple Tree' gallows, 1607.*

The Triple Tree labelled 'Tyborne' can be seen north-west of the City of London (detail above). Its presence on numerous maps demonstrates that the distinctive triangular gallows was a significant London landmark.

MAP BY JOHN NORDEN, PUBLISHED IN WILLIAM CAMDEN'S BRITANNIA, 1637 EDITION.

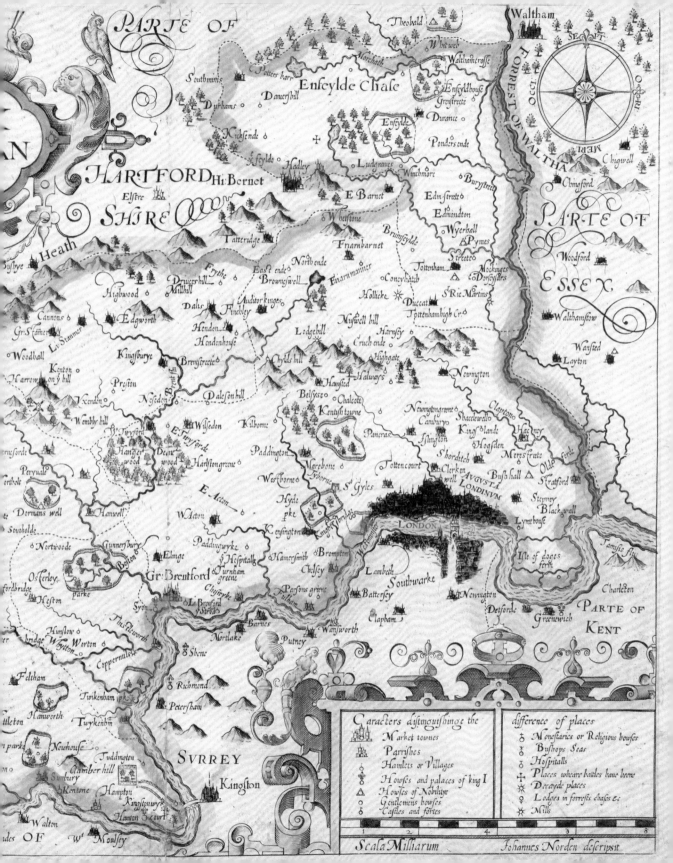

PROTESTANT MARTYR

Anne Askew, aged 24, executed on 16 July 1546

Anne Askew was a writer and poet from Lincolnshire. Her study of the Bible convinced her to become a devout Protestant, and speak out against the established doctrine of the Church. She is said to have demanded a divorce from her Catholic husband before moving to London. Her beliefs and preaching led to her arrest in May 1546 and she endured the torture of being stretched on the rack at the Tower of London without renouncing her faith or denouncing her associates. Her injuries from the rack meant that she had to be carried on a chair to Smithfield, where she was burned to death with three other Protestants. She is one of only two women recorded as having been both tortured at the Tower of London and burned at the stake. Bishop Nicholas Shaxton had been condemned with Anne but had recanted and been granted a reprieve. He was sent to preach the sermon from the pulpit at her execution, offering her a final chance to repent. Askew's faith, however, was unwavering. She disputed the bishop's biblical interpretation and unrepentantly went to her death.

← *Anne Askew and other Protestant martyrs being burned at the stake at Smithfield, 16 July 1546.* Askew was burned along with John Adams, Nicholas Belenian and John Lascelles (Lacels). In this image, the pyres are being prepared around the base of the stakes to which the condemned have already been tied. Bishop Shaxton is shown preaching from the pulpit to the left.

WOODCUT, PUBLISHED IN FOXE'S BOOK OF MARTYRS, 1610.

NEWGATE

Between 1690 and 1780, criminals who committed crimes inside or close to Newgate were sometimes executed outside the prison as a warning to others. In December 1783, the open space outside the Debtors' Door on the street called Old Bailey became London's principal site of public execution. Here a scaffold was erected with the 'new drop' (trapdoor) gallows featuring two parallel beams from which up to twelve people could hang. By 1868, at least 1,130 men and women had been executed on this spot.

THE TOWER OF LONDON AND TOWER HILL

A small number of noble and royal men and women, as well as a few soldiers and spies, have been executed within the walls of the Tower of London, thereby affording them a degree of privacy. Many more – at least 120 between 1388 and 1780 – were executed in public on Tower Hill. Beheadings and occasionally hangings were frequent enough for the 'posts of the scaffold' to become a landmark. Executions of prominent political figures, such as Thomas Wentworth, Earl of Strafford (beheaded in 1641), or of high-profile traitors, such as the leaders of the Jacobite rebellion (beheaded in 1746), attracted huge crowds of spectators to Tower Hill.

↓ *Relic from Newgate Prison.*
This keystone, placed in a souvenir frame, formed part of the archway over the Debtors' Door of Newgate Prison through which the condemned walked to the scaffold. The prison finally closed in 1902 and was demolished two years later. There was considerable public interest in its relics, which were sold at auction.

→ *Map showing the Tower of London and surrounding area, 1597.*

This map was produced as part of a survey of the area around the Tower, known as the Liberties of the Tower. The posts of the scaffold on Tower Hill are marked to the northwest of the Tower (detail above). The site is marked today with a memorial. A further memorial to those executed inside the Tower can be found at Tower Green, close to St Peter ad Vincula, the church within the Tower precincts.

MAP BY GULIELMUS HAIWARD AND J. GASCOYNE IN 1597, PUBLISHED BY THE SOCIETY OF ANTIQUARIES OF LONDON, 1742.

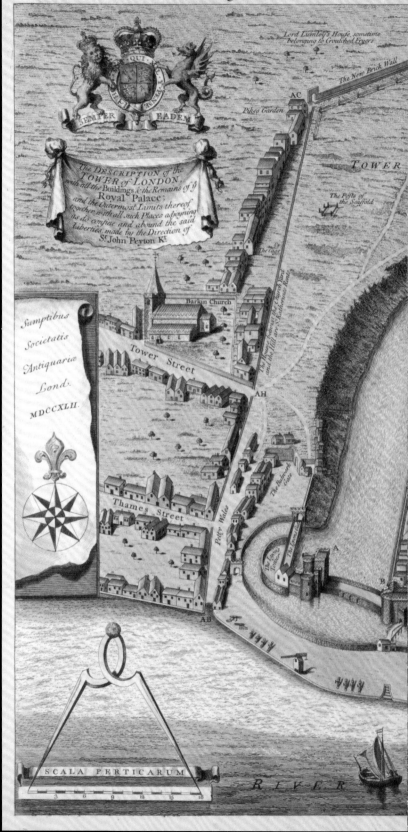

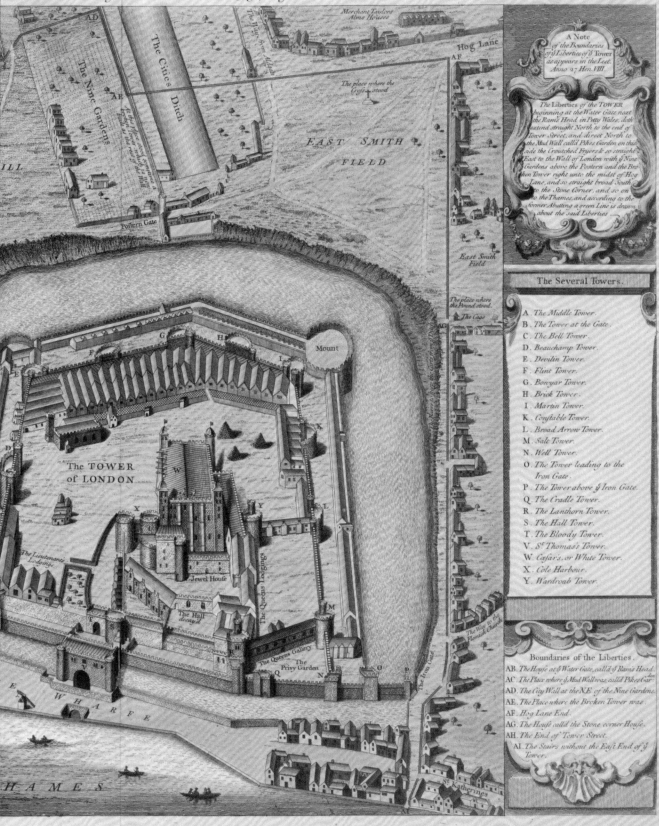

KENNINGTON COMMON AND HORSEMONGER LANE

South of the River Thames, the Surrey Gallows was located on Kennington Common, just 100 metres from where Oval Underground station now stands. From at least 1678 until 1800, this was the principal execution site for the county of Surrey, with others in Guildford and Kingston. In 1799, building work on the new Surrey County Gaol at Horsemonger Lane in Southwark was completed. From 1800, most executions in Surrey occurred here, with public executions taking place on the roof of the gaol gatehouse, making them highly visible to spectators. The gallows used the 'new drop' method and could dispatch seven people at once, as happened twice in 1803. In total, 126 people were publicly executed at the prison, with five more being hanged there privately between 1868 and 1877. One of the most famous executions at Horsemonger Lane was that of husband and wife Frederick and Maria Manning, in 1849, for the murder of Maria's lover, Patrick O'Connor. They were hanged together.

↑ *Execution outside Newgate Prison, 1809.*
The Debtors' Door entrance to the Prison can be seen at the back of the scaffold, with chains and shackles hanging above it. The condemned arrived on the scaffold through this door.

ENGRAVING, PUBLISHED BY NUTTALL, FISHER AND CO., 1809.

REBEL LORDS

*William Boyd, 4th Earl of Kilmarnock, aged 41,
and Arthur Elphinstone, 6th Lord Balmerino, aged 58,
executed on 18 August 1746*

Kilmarnock and Balmerino were Scottish peers and members of the Jacobite army that fought against British government forces to depose King George II and restore Charles Edward Stuart, the Young Pretender, to the throne. They were both captured at the Battle of Culloden in 1746, tried in London, where they were found guilty of treason, and sentenced to be drawn, hanged and quartered, although this was commuted to beheading. Their execution took place on Tower Hill on 18 August 1746, and thousands of people came to watch, thronging the streets, stands and rooftops around the scaffold, while 'patterers' sold execution broadsides (cheaply printed accounts of the crime and execution), oranges and drinks.

Spectators were impressed by the calm demeanour of the Scottish lords. Killmarnock was executed first and expressed contrition for his actions. Balmerino, however, affirmed his commitment to Charles Edward Stuart, having declared, 'If I had a thousand lives, I would lay them all down in the same cause.' Kilmarnock and Balmerino had requested that four men attend the execution holding a scarlet cloth in which to catch their severed heads on the scaffold.

↓ *Beheading of the rebel
lords on Tower Hill,
18 August 1746.*
HAND-COLOURED ETCHING,
PUBLISHED BY ROBERT
WILKINSON, 1746.

← *The execution of Jacobite rebels on Kennington Common, 30 July 1746.*

This print depicts the drawing, hanging, quartering and burning of Francis Towneley and other members of the Manchester Regiment of Jacobites. The executioner holds up the head of one of the rebels while a dismembered arm burns in the fire. Two hooded, tartan-clad soldiers hang from the gallows.

ENGRAVING, AFTER SAMUEL WALE FOR THE TYBURN CHRONICLE, 1768.

← *Foundation stone of the Surrey County Gaol, 1799.*

The inscription warns that 'any person trespassing [...] will be prosecuted.'

EXECUTION DOCK

From 1360 to 1834, crimes committed at sea, including piracy, murder, mutiny and treason, were tried by the High Court of Admiralty. On execution day, capital convicts were led from Marshalsea or Newgate Prison to Execution Dock in Wapping, on the banks of the River Thames. There they were hanged on a gallows erected on the foreshore at low tide. The bodies remained until three tides had washed over them, a practice that ended in the late 18th century. The crowds that attended such executions can be seen in the watercolour William Clift painted of John Gillam and William Brockman's hanging in 1816. The pair were smugglers who had killed four revenue officers. They were sentenced to be dissected after death, and then displayed in a gibbet on the Kent coast. The last executions at Execution Dock were of William Watts and George Davis

↑ *Silver tipstaff, 1796.*
Tipstaves were carried by the Admiralty bailiffs who escorted the condemned to Execution Dock. The base unscrews to reveal a silver oar, the symbol of the Admiralty. This tipstaff is engraved 'R.M. in acknowledgement of long & valuable services 1796'.

THE PERSECUTION OF JEWS IN MEDIEVAL ENGLAND

The Jewish community of medieval England was frequently subjected to hostility and discrimination. In 1255, 92 Jews were held at the Tower after being falsely accused of murdering a young boy, Hugh of Lincoln. On 22 November that year, eighteen of the prisoners were drawn through London's streets and hanged. Between 1278 and 1279, 600 Jews from across the country were accused of coinage offences and sent to the Tower. The crime of coinage or coin clipping was widespread in the 13th century. The edges of English coins, made from high-quality silver, were frequently snipped off to be melted down into other items. Although more Christians than Jews carried out coinage crimes at this time, Jews were more likely to be punished by hanging, owing to religious prejudices. Only 29 Christians were executed during 1278–79, compared with 269 Jews, who were hanged at Tower Hill.

↑ *Clipped silver 'short cross' penny, 1216–47.*
'Short cross' pennies were especially vulnerable to clipping, as the cross did not reach the edge of the coin.

← *Pirate hanging at Execution Dock, Wapping.*

On the left of the image, the Admiralty Marshal is on horseback holding the Admiralty oar mace. The church in the background, on the opposite side of the River Thames, is St Mary's in Rotherhithe.

ENGRAVING BY PAGE AFTER ROBERT DODD, PUBLISHED IN THE MALEFACTOR'S REGISTER, 1779.

for piracy in 1830, at which time it was noted that it had been ten years since the previous execution there.

The procession to Execution Dock was led by the Admiralty Marshal who carried the Admiralty oar mace, an ornate silver oar. The mace was a ceremonial symbol of the Admiralty Court's authority and is still in use today, present at sittings of the Court. Admiralty bailiffs escorted the procession carrying tipstaves as

a sign of their authority. Despite these escorts, the condemned sometimes escaped. Newspapers of the 18th century reported individuals being cut down from the gallows alive by 'seafaring persons' and spirited away by boat.

OTHER PUBLIC EXECUTION SITES

In addition to the customary execution sites in London, public execution sometimes took place in other open spaces, such as at Charing Cross, or Cheapside in the City of London. During the 16th and 17th centuries, several locations around the Palace of Westminster were used for public execution and the display of body parts, and for placing people in the pillory (stocks). After the restoration of the monarchy in 1660, King Charles II ordered the bodies of Oliver Cromwell, John Bradshaw and Henry Ireton, all of whom had died natural deaths, to be exhumed. All three were among the leading 'regicides' who had signed the death warrant of his father, King Charles I. They had been buried at Westminster Abbey and Charles ordered their bodies to be dug up, executed and decapitated. This was done on 30 January 1661, the

↑ The hanging of John Gillam and William Brockman at Execution Dock, 31 January 1816.

The execution was witnessed by William Clift, conservator and illustrator at the Royal College of Surgeons, who painted this watercolour from memory. The gallows is a tiny detail at the centre of the picture which is otherwise dominated by the thousands of spectators crowded together along the shore and in boats to witness the event.

WATERCOLOUR BY WILLIAM CLIFT, 1816.

TREASONOUS COLLABORATORS

*William Cundell and John Smith,
executed on 16 March 1812*

William Cundell and John Smith were among some 50 British sailors who collaborated with their French captors on the island of Mauritius during the Napoleonic Wars in 1808. When the island fell to the British, 38 of the 50 escaped with the French, while twelve surrendered. The men who surrendered were returned to Britain and put on trial at the Surrey County Sessions House. Seven were found guilty of high treason and, of these, five were pardoned and transported to the colonies and two, Cundell and Smith, condemned. They received the traditional traitors' sentence of being drawn, hanged and quartered, which took place at Surrey County Gaol, Horsemonger Lane on 16 March 1812. The two men were drawn across the yard on a hurdle, and hanged until dead before being decapitated. The Attorney General 'pitied the situation of the unfortunate men' but regarded the punishment as necessary 'to deter others from forsaking their duty'. Contemporary accounts describe the crowd at the execution as dissolving into tears at the fate of the two young men.

An Exact Representation of the Execution of WM. CUNDELL & J. SMITH for High Treason at the County Goal Horse-monger-lane Surry MONDAY MARCH 16th 1812

← *The execution of William Cundell and John Smith at Surrey County Gaol, Horsemonger Lane, 16 March 1812.*
ETCHING, 1812.

anniversary of the execution of King Charles I, and their heads were displayed on poles outside Westminster Hall, the scene of his trial. Cromwell's head remained there until 1685 when it blew down in a storm, and later passed through various owners before finally being buried in a secret location in Sidney Sussex College, Cambridge in 1960.

Charing Cross was used for executions during the 16th and 17th centuries and afterwards as a place to pillory criminals. In 1660, the diarist Samuel Pepys witnessed Major-General Harrison, another of the 'regicides' of King Charles I, being drawn, hanged and quartered: 'Thus it was my chance to see the King beheaded at White Hall, and to see the first bloodshed in revenge [...] at Charing Cross.' A statue of the King was placed there in 1675 and marks the spot to this day.

Temporary gallows were erected on several occasions at Cheapside between the 14th and 17th centuries. In 1554, they were in place for over 100 days following the execution of two of the rebels involved in a Protestant uprising against Queen Mary I. On 8 May (or 8 April in some accounts), a dead cat, dressed up to

↑ *The heads of Cromwell, Bradshaw and Ireton on poles outside Westminster Hall, 30 January 1661.*

The scene at Tyburn, where the bodies were hanged and then decapitated, is shown in the foreground of this engraving. In the background, the heads of Cromwell (1), Bradshaw (2) and Ireton (3) can be seen on poles above Westminster Hall.

ENGRAVING, 1700–50.

resemble a priest or monk, was found strung up on the scaffold. This anti-Catholic protest was presumably intended to subvert the intended symbolism of the gallows that had been left in Cheapside as a warning to other rebels.

SITES OF CRIME

It was not unusual for criminals to be hanged close to the site of their crime. This could act both as a comfort to those living nearby who wanted to see justice done, and as a deterrent to any locals considering similar crimes. William Flower was a Protestant martyr who was burned at the stake in St Margaret's churchyard in 1555. The manner and location of his punishment were selected to fit his crime: he had attacked a priest in St Margaret's Church with a knife, badly injuring him. After first having his hand cut off, Flower burned to death very slowly as insufficient fuel was used in the fire. Eventually he had to be pulled down into the fire to burn.

In 1663, Colonel James Turner was hanged at the Leadenhall Street end of Lime Street for burgling a merchant's house in Lime Street. Samuel Pepys attended this execution, as well as several others; on this occasion, he paid 'a shilling to stand upon the wheel of a cart, in great pain, above an houre [sic] before the execution was done', and later, at a coffee house, learned that

↑ The Pillory,
Charing Cross, 1809.
Two figures stand in the pillory, with the equestrian statue of King Charles I, which still stands at Charing Cross, to the right.
ETCHING BY CHARLES AUGUSTE PUGIN AND THOMAS ROWLANDSON WITH AQUATINT BY JOHN BLUCK, PUBLISHED BY RUDOLPH ACKERMANN, 1809.

→ A dead cat,
suspended from the
Cheapside gallows, 1554.
This was very clearly an anti-Catholic message: the cat was dressed in robes similar to a priest's, with the top of its head shaven like a monk's. A circular piece of paper had been placed between its paws, symbolising a consecrated wafer or host.
ENGRAVING, PUBLISHED IN THE NEW AND COMPLETE BOOK OF MARTYRS, 1784.

The Popish party astonished in the morning of May 8, 1554, on finding in Cheapside a CAT suspended on a Gallows, habited like a Monk with a shaven Crown &c. on which account Q. Mary and the Papists were highly incensed against the Protestants of London.

Turner had 'delayed the time by discourses and prayers [...] in hope of a reprieve; but none came'. Local executions became more common in the 18th century. In 1733, Sarah Malcolm was condemned to death for involvement in the robbery and murder of three women in the Temple Chambers, near Fleet Street. According to the 'Account' of the chaplain of Newgate (called the Ordinary), 'because of the atrociousness of her crimes and for terror to other wickedly disposed people, [she] was appointed to be executed in Fleet-street, at a place nigh where her heinous crimes were committed.'

Rioters and rebels were also executed locally as a warning to their associates, although often their notoriety attracted onlookers from miles around. In 1780, the anti-Catholic 'Gordon

↑ The burning of William Flower in St Margaret's Churchyard, Westminster, 24 April 1555.

Flower holds up his bleeding stump to the assembled crowd – his hand has been mounted onto a soldier's halberd. Although the pyre being prepared looks quite large here, accounts of his death said that there was insufficient fuel.

ENGRAVING BY THOMAS BOWLES, 1746–55.

Riots' resulted in the hanging of 22 men and four women at thirteen locations in London for the destruction of property during the riots. When the executions began in July 1780, the first to be hanged was William Pateman on Coleman Street, close to the house that he had been found guilty of helping to partly demolish. Other executions took place outside Newgate Prison, which had been damaged in a successful attempt to liberate detained rioters. The magistrates' decision to disperse the executions across London both avoided a mass public execution at one site (Tyburn), and the possibility of further mob violence, and also ensured that local people saw justice done locally. The punishments were swift and severe and sought to deter future unrest.

One of the last people to be publicly executed at the site of their crime in London was John Cashman, a sailor, in 1816. He was found guilty of stealing guns from the shop of a Mr Beckwith on Snow Hill, during the Spa Fields riots in December of that year. Interestingly, and understandably, Beckwith didn't want the execution to take place outside his house and he twice appealed to the Secretary of State's office. His request, however, was turned down and Cashman was hanged there on 12 March 1817.

↑ *Execution of Colonel James Turner at the Leadenhall Street end of Lime Street, 1663.*
WOODCUT, C.1663.

THE EXECUTION OF KING CHARLES I

'...after a little pause, the King stretching forth his hands, the Executioner at one blow, severed his head from his body.'

Anonymous, 1649

King Charles I had a fractious relationship with Parliament, which disagreed with many of his policies and wanted to curb his power. In 1642, the King's failed attempt to arrest five MPs for treason led to angry protests against him in London. He fled the capital and the country was plunged into civil war, with Royalist armies fighting those of Parliament. While being held prisoner by Parliament, Charles secretly arranged that a Scottish army would invade England to help him regain his throne. In an extraordinary act by Parliament, Charles was put on trial for treason and convicted of 'High Treason and other high Crymes'. His death warrant was signed by 59 men, including Oliver Cromwell who later ruled the country as Lord Protector. The King was sentenced 'to be putt to death by the severinge of his head from his body'.

Execution at Banqueting House, Whitehall
The death warrant specified where the execution was to take place: 'In the open streete [sic] before Whitehall'. Whitehall was chosen as the location for the execution on 30 January 1649 both for very personal and very public reasons. The palace of Whitehall had been Charles's home for much of his reign, and it meant that he would walk to his death through rooms that he knew intimately. At the same time, the sumptuous and expensive Banqueting House, built for his father, King

↑ *Portrait of Charles I as a Martyr King.*
OIL ON CANVAS, BRITISH SCHOOL, C.1660–70.

James I and completed by Charles, had become a symbol of his oppressive rule and his belief in the divine right of kings. A stage was built out into the street from the first floor of Banqueting Hall, creating a public

Endhaupfung deß Konigs in Engelandt Ano 1649.

theatre for this first state execution of a monarch in England's history. However, the street location, surrounded by the palace's buildings, also meant that the crowd could not be too large and so the chances of rioting were lessened. Nonetheless, an eyewitness claimed that, at the moment the King was beheaded, 'there was such a groan by the thousands then present as I never heard before and desire I may never hear again'.

After his execution, Charles's body 'was immediately coffin'd, and covered with a black Velvet-Pall' and then embalmed. He was buried in St George's Chapel Windsor nine days later.

↑ *German print showing King Charles I's execution, 30 January 1649.*

The shocking news of the King's death was reported across Europe. This print shows the executioner and his assistant, both masked, having just cut off Charles's head with an axe and holding it up to the crowd. The print would have been illegal in England as it shows a woman fainting and other people crying. It was a crime to 'speak, preach or write against' the King's execution.

ENGRAVING, 1649–1800.

THE KING'S RELICS

For some, the King was regarded as a martyr, and a trade grew up around the personal possessions or relics associated with his death. Supporters of King Charles I who could not get hold of actual relics from his execution bought jewels in his memory. They were painted with his portrait and symbols of mortality, such as a skull or coffin.

The Museum of London's collection contains several garments reputedly worn or carried by Charles at his execution. Their material and style indicate they are of the correct date and quality to have been owned by the King, although there are conflicting accounts of what he wore on the day of execution, and what happened to those items after his death.

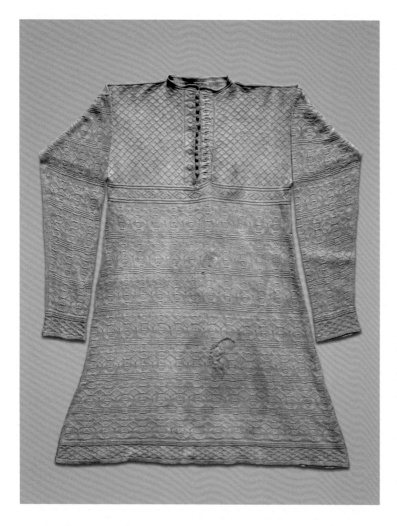

← *Knitted silk vest, mid 17th century.*
King Charles I's attendant, Sir Thomas Herbert, reported that the King wore an extra shirt on the morning he was beheaded in order not to shiver in the cold January air. He did not want people to think he was afraid, declaring, 'I fear not Death!' Made from silk, this finely knitted undergarment (or 'waistcoat', as it was called at the time) was a warm, luxurious and expensive item, fit for a king.

The London Museum acquired the undergarment in 1924, along with a note claiming it had been worn by Charles at his execution and 'from the Scaffold came into the Hands of Doctor Hobbs, his physician who attended him upon that Occasion'. The vest remained in the physician's family until the late 19th century, when it was sold and resold several times.

Analysis of the stains on the vest have been carried out in the past but the results were inconclusive. The stains fluoresced under ultraviolet light, indicating they could be from body fluids like sweat or vomit, or even food and drink. Blood stains should turn black under UV light but after this length of time, this reaction might no longer occur.

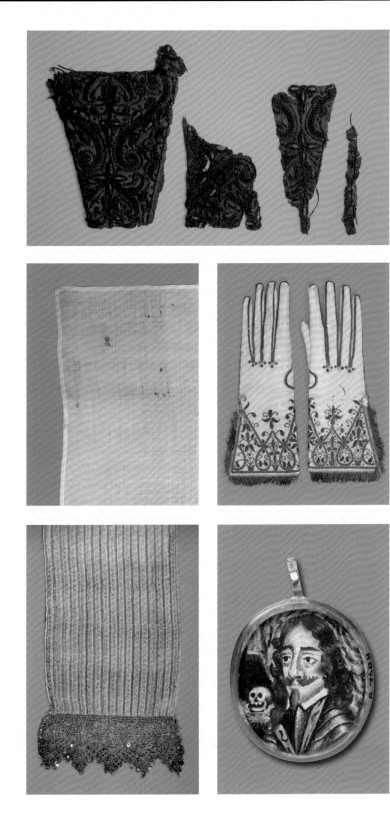

← *Four fragments of a cloak, mid 17th century.*

According to the note donated with these fragments, they are all that remain of a black cloak Charles gave to his attendant, Sir Thomas Herbert, before the King passed through a passage that led from Banqueting House to the scaffold erected outside. One of Herbert's daughters supposedly gave the cloak to Countess Johanna Sophia of Hohenlohe-Langenburg, who was based at the English royal court in the early 18th century.

← *Gloves, early to mid 17th century.*

These fine leather gloves with silver embroidery are said to have been given by King Charles I to Bishop Juxon, who accompanied him to his execution. Several pairs of gloves have the same supposed origin. Embellished gloves like this were popular gifts. Charles's wardrobe accounts list more than 1,000 pairs, suggesting that the King often presented them to others.

← *Handkerchief (detail), mid 17th century.*

This handkerchief is embroidered with the royal cypher – the King's initials, 'CR', in red silk, with a crown above. The letters stand for Carolus Rex, the Latin for King Charles. The handkerchief is made of very fine linen but is otherwise unusually plain for a royal accessory.

← *Memorial pendant of King Charles I, mid 17th century.*

← *Sash (detail), c.1625–50.*

Made from silk and metal thread, this sash is said to have been associated with Charles, but the connection to the King cannot be proven. Decorated with silver-gilt lace and spangles, the sash would have been a very expensive, high-status item, worn across the body or around the waist, over a doublet or coat.

PREPARING FOR EXECUTION

By the 18th century, most people who committed capital offences in London faced a trial at the Old Bailey. Even if death sentences were imposed, they were not inevitable. It was common for prisoners to petition the monarch to ask for a reprieve, and many were granted. As there were so many capital crimes by the late 1700s, the justice system depended on reprieves to reduce the number of executions to a manageable level. For those who were not reprieved, there were usually only a few days remaining before they faced the executioner.

Letters, diaries and published accounts reveal the intense emotional strain and fear of public execution felt by the condemned during their final days and hours. Many frantically wrote letters to their loved ones, or organised petitions professing their innocence; others turned to drink and some resorted to taking their own lives to avoid their fate. Each condemned prisoner was encouraged to repent and to accept religious and moral instruction from the prison chaplain.

TRIALS AND THE OLD BAILEY

All serious crimes committed in London north of the River Thames were tried at the Old Bailey court, named after the street in which it stands. It was originally built as a courtroom adjoining the medieval Newgate Prison to serve the City of London and the county of Middlesex. In the 19th century, its jurisdiction was extended to include the trials of major cases from the rest of England.

Trials at the Old Bailey were – and still are – open to the public, although the available space was diminished during the 18th and 19th centuries, and spectators were charged an entrance fee. As today, lengthy queues would form for the most infamous or salacious cases. Those unable to attend could read about the details in the Old Bailey proceedings or in newspaper reports, which were circulated around the country and abroad, ensuring that justice was seen to be served. Trials were quick, and people could be sentenced to death in less than an hour.

Until the early 19th century, lawyers were rarely in court. The case was brought by the prosecutor, who was often also the victim of the crime, the defendant defended themselves, and witnesses were called. Originally, only the prosecution could call witnesses but, from 1702, the defence could too. The judge questioned those involved and meted out the punishment, once the jury had considered the case and passed judgement. For the most serious crimes, the judge was the Recorder of London, the most senior judge at the Old Bailey and a City of London appointment. If juries took too long in making a decision, they could be kept without food, water or heat until they did. Juries were all male until 1920.

The majority of condemned prisoners were held at the notoriously squalid Newgate Prison while they awaited execution. Some had weeks to prepare, pray and say farewell to friends and family; others had only days. Sentences were often

↓ Dispatch bag badge, c.1850.

This badge was used on the dispatch bag that carried death warrants from the Home Office to Newgate Prison in the mid 19th century. It bears the coat of arms of the City of London and the word 'Newgate'. Prisoners would have awaited the arrival of this bag with dread.

carried out with what seems to modern eyes as alarming speed. The Murder Act 1752 stipulated that those guilty of murder had to be executed two days after sentencing, or three days if the second day was a Sunday. In 1767, for example, Elizabeth Brownrigg was sentenced to death on Saturday 12 September and executed on Monday 14 September.

DEATH SENTENCES

When passing the death sentence, the judge first placed a small square of black cloth on their head, on top of their judicial wig. This was the 'black cap', a tradition that continued in Britain until the abolition of the death penalty in 1969 (although the black cap remains part of High Court judges' ceremonial robes). It was an action that denoted the seriousness of the moment, usually bringing a solemnity to the court that may not have been there before.

Women were far less likely than men to be sentenced to death. This was largely due to gender stereotypes; men were perceived to be stronger, more aggressive and more prone to violence, and women as more emotional, weaker and more compliant. In

↑ *A trial at the Central Criminal Court, the Old Bailey, 1835.*
The judges' bench is at the centre with the barristers and clerks below. The jury are seated to the left; at this time, they would have deliberated in situ. The empty dock is in the foreground. The man in the blue jacket to the left, taking notes, is probably an official scribe or clerk.
WATERCOLOUR BY THOMAS HOSMER SHEPHERD, 1835.

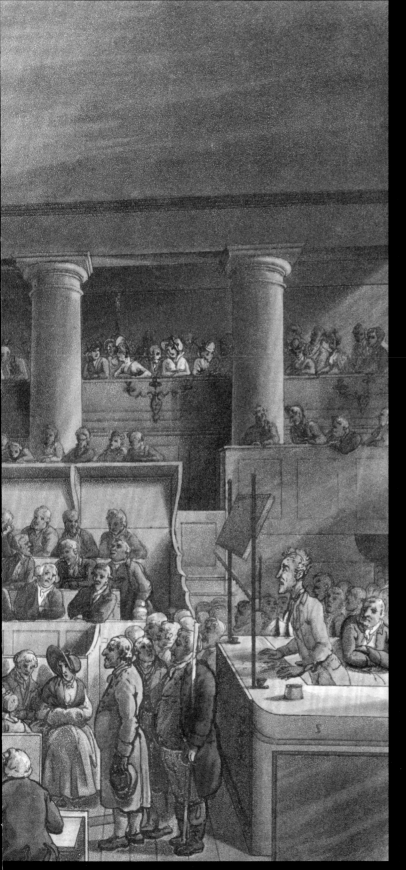

← *Old Bailey, 1809.*
In this scene a female witness, in a white dress, is addressing the judge. She stands beneath a sounding board on a pole which would have helped to amplify her voice. The accused stands in the dock to the right. Above his head is a mirrored reflector to shine the daylight from the large windows onto his face.

ETCHING BY CHARLES PUGIN AND THOMAS ROWLANDSON WITH AQUATINT BY JOSEPH CONSTANTINE STADLER, PUBLISHED BY RUDOLPH ACKERMANN, 1809.

London & Middlesex } To the Sheriffs of the City of London, And,

To the Sheriff of the County of Middlesex, And,

To the Keeper of His Majesty's Gaol of Newgate

Whereas at the Session of Gaol delivery of Newgate for the City of London and County of Middlesex holden at Justice Hall in the Old Bailey on Wednesday the thirteenth day of December last in Francis Onion otherwise Bates, James Dobson, Samuel Phipps, William Bead, George Wallace, James Watts, Francis Hardy, John Gerwalt, William Allen, John Wright, Joseph Morrell, Frederick Daniel Lucas, Edward Ham, Joseph Reary, James Brown, William Adams, William Jones, Henry Staples, John Turner, Joseph Mander, Robert Horsley, Dennis Sullivan, and Jacob Abrahams received sentence of death for the respective Offences in their several Indictments mentioned And whereas also at the Session of Gaol delivery of Newgate holden as aforesaid on Wednesday the tenth day of January last Thomas Glaves and Joseph Crawley amongst others received sentence of death for the respective Offences in their Indictments mentioned Now it is hereby ordered that in execution of the said sentence be made and done upon them the said Frederick Daniel Lucas, Edward Ham, Samuel Phipps, James Brown, Joseph Crawley, Dennis Sullivan, William Adams, William Jones, Henry Staples, John Turner, Joseph Mander, Robert Horsley, and James Dobson on Wednesday next the fourteenth day of this instant month of February at the place of Execution before His Majesty's Gaol of Newgate And it is His Majesty's commands that Execution of the said sentence upon them the said John Gerwalt James Watts, Francis Hardy, Francis Onion otherwise Bates, William Bead, George Wallace, William Allen, Thomas Glaves, Joseph Reary, John Wright, Joseph Morrell, and Jacob Abrahams be respited until His Majesty's pleasure touching them be further known

Given under my hand and Seal this ninth day of February One thousand seven hundred and eighty seven

James Adair
Recorder

general, this meant that women received less harsh sentences than men, although women found guilty of particularly violent or heinous crimes could be punished more severely. There was a public fascination with such crimes and with the women who transgressed the perceived predetermined order of things. In 1849, when Maria Manning was found guilty of murder with her husband, a lawyer at the trial claimed that when a woman 'gives way to vice, she sinks far lower' than a man. A condemned woman who was expecting a child could 'plead her belly'. A jury of matrons would examine her and, if they upheld her pregnancy, her sentence would be respited (delayed) until after the birth of her child. In reality, once the baby was born, most women were reprieved. From 1848, pregnant women were always granted a permanent reprieve, although it was only in 1931 that the death penalty for pregnant women was legally abolished.

PETITIONS FOR MERCY

After judges sentenced criminals to death, their cases were reviewed by the King or Queen in Council, a meeting of the monarch with the home secretary, ministers and advisors. They read notes from the judge and petitions for mercy and decided who would live or die. The injustice of the swift trial system at the Old Bailey encouraged the condemned to send in such petitions. Frequently, there were only days between sentencing and execution, so petitions and character references were hurriedly drawn up, often by legal representatives, and signed by acquaintances, family members and even prosecutors and jurors concerned at the role they played in the conviction. The Home Office sent death warrants back to prisons where staff would tell the inmates of their fate. It was a terrifying lottery that depended on many factors, including the mood of people at the council meeting and how many criminals had been convicted of the same crime at once.

Most petitions were written in desperation, representing the final attempt to save a life. Joseph Harwood, a highway robber convicted in 1824, was aged 18, and his petition was signed by his illiterate mother with a simple cross. The letter of petition says it was sworn at the Mansion House in front of the Mayor, indicating that it was probably written out for Harwood's mother by a clerk or official at the Mansion House. A humble seller of washing lines, he was, according to the petition, led astray by bad company who took advantage of him while drunk. With no well-

← Death warrant and stay of execution for prisoners at Newgate Prison, 9 February 1787. This death warrant orders the execution of thirteen prisoners outside Newgate on 14 February 1787, for their crimes of highway robbery and burglary. A further twelve prisoners have been respited until the king has made a final decision. The warrant is signed by the Recorder of London, the senior judge at the Old Bailey.

← *The Lord Mayor of London with a petition to reprieve condemned prisoners.* The Right Honourable John Thomas Thorpe, Lord Mayor of London (1820–1), shown here in his court dress, standing before the bars of Newgate Prison and holding a petition to reprieve seventeen prisoners. Petitions signed by officials such as Thorpe were often more successful than those without such endorsements.

WATERCOLOUR BY JOHN DEMPSEY, 1820.

connected supporters, Harwood's petition failed. The Ordinary of Newgate described him as being 'dreadfully distressed' prior to his execution.

REPRIEVES

Youths, first offenders and those with local support or influential contacts were most likely to be reprieved, their sentences usually commuted to transportation to the overseas penal colonies. In 1827, Thomas Sackett, aged 31, robbed a bank clerk. Born into a respectable Essex family, he arrived in London having

'Joseph Harwood was a youth of honest and industrious habits and if the offence [...] were committed by him, it was [...] at the instigation of Persons who took advantage of his being in a state of intoxication.'

Affidavit in support of Joseph Harwood's petition for mercy, 16 November 1824 already lost a substantial inheritance. He set up a butcher's shop in Whitechapel, but his fortunes further declined when he was convicted of robbery. Sackett submitted a bundle of petitions signed by Essex businessmen and civic officials, including the Mayor of Colchester. His influential petitioners helped secure a reprieve and he was transported to Australia, where he died in 1837. Another example of a successful petition was that of Matthew Verney, aged 45. In 1822, he was convicted of stealing a horse and sentenced to death. His petition referred to his insanity caused by a fractured skull at the age of 15 and was supported by an attached note from St Luke's Hospital for the Insane confirming his two previous periods of confinement there. Verney was reprieved and sent to the prison hulk *Retribution*, which was moored at Woolwich. His planned transportation never took place on account of his mental condition and, in 1827, he was transferred to Bethlem psychiatric hospital. Those newly arrived in London from other parts of the country or overseas were less likely to have access to respected local contacts who could support petitions. According to the Old Bailey's records approximately 60 per cent of those sentenced to death in the 18th century were pardoned, rising to about 90 per cent in the 1830s.

In Newgate Prison, the news about who had been reprieved and who was to be executed was delivered by the Ordinary, who read the Recorder's Report to the condemned prisoners. On 25 May 1824, the Reverend Dr Horace Cotton, Ordinary of Newgate, and William Box, the prison's surgeon, recorded their visit to the condemned prisoners in the Newgate Visitors' Book and described the reactions of the condemned upon learning their fate. Cotton 'communicated the dreadfull intelligence' that two of the 43 men in the condemned cell would be executed. He told the condemned women that they were all reprieved and wrote that '2 were in fits, the rest wept incessantly'. Prisoners continued to share a cell after the announcement, leading to feelings of guilt, jealousy and anger.

↑ *A condemned man being reprieved on his way to Tyburn.*
The prisoner is being released from the cart that was transporting him to the gallows, having received his reprieve.
ENGRAVING, C.1795.

JOHN SMITH *cut down at* TYBURN, *in consequence of a reprieve which came five Minutes after he had been turned off.*

It was not unknown, especially in the late 17th century, for reprieves to arrive after the condemned had set off on their procession to the gallows, meaning that many held out hope for a last-minute stay of execution. 'Last dying speeches' purporting to record the final words of the condemned were sometimes printed and sold before the news of a reprieve was broadcast, making them untrustworthy sources of information.

NEWGATE PRISON

The origins of Newgate Prison date back to the late 12th century. It was destroyed in the Great Fire of London in 1666, by which time it was notorious for its filth and overcrowding, and rebuilt by Sir Christopher Wren. A substantial expansion was undertaken between 1767 and 1782, to designs by George Dance the Younger. This redesign was interrupted in 1780 by the anti-Catholic Gordon Riots, during which the prison was burned down and 117 prisoners released. The new prison, although an improvement on its predecessor, was a large, rather forbidding structure. Dance positioned authentic chains and shackles over the entrance known as the Debtors' Door, symbols of suffering and a harsh confinement that were intended to instil reflection and terror in all who passed by the prison. For most of its life, Newgate housed both a debtors' prison and a gaol for criminals,

↑ *Dr Cotton announcing the Death Warrant, 1826.*
This watercolour, made by a prisoner, William Thomson, demonstrates the relief of those reprieved and the despair of those condemned.

All the Prisoners to the amount of 300 were released this Night.

The Devastations occasioned by the RIOTERS of LOND and burning Mr Akerman's Furn

Hamilton delin.

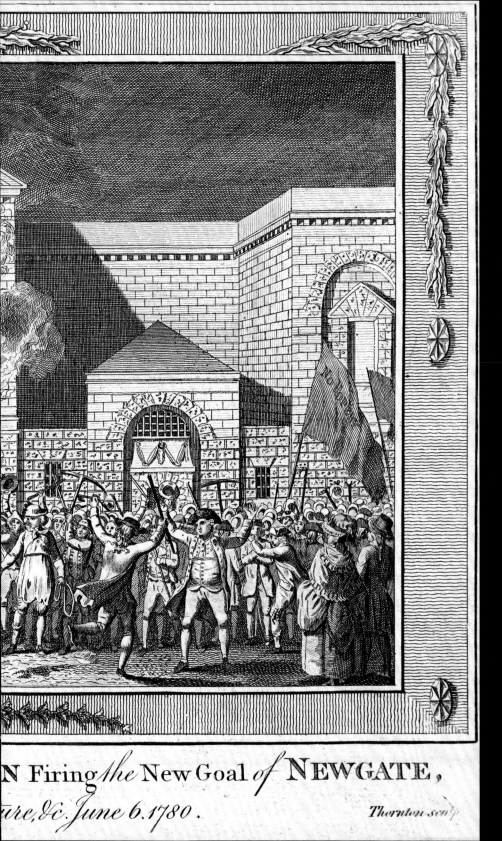

N Firing *the* New Goal *of* NEWGATE,

ure, &c. June 6.1780.

Thornton *sculp*

← *Rioters attacking Newgate Prison and burning the Governor's furniture, 6 June 1780.*

Estimates as to how many prisoners were released varied widely, from the 300 mentioned on this engraving to the official list of 117 named individuals that appeared a few days later.

ENGRAVING BY T. THORNTON
AFTER WILLIAM HAMILTON,
PUBLISHED BY ALEXANDER
HOGG, 1780.

including those condemned to death. Things improved slightly once the debtors were moved out after 1815. However, in 1817, the Governor noted the 'dilapidated and dangerous state' of the prison roof which 'requires immediate Repairs for the safety of the Persons confined'. In 1850, William Hepworth Dixon described the prison as 'massive, dark and solemn', one of the few buildings in London to have a 'character'. It was finally closed in 1902 and was demolished in 1904 to make way for the new Central Criminal Court, which is still known today as the Old Bailey.

The number of inmates at Newgate was ever-fluctuating. As well as the condemned, the prison held those on trial at the Old Bailey, the reprieved awaiting transportation and the convicted before their transferral to other prisons. For example, on 4 March 1817 the Governor of Newgate listed the number of 'capital convicts under sentence of death' as 48 men and seven women; a further 50 men and eleven women had been respited and 172 people were to be transported to penal colonies.

Throughout the 18th and early 19th centuries, visitors and others noted the over-crowding and poor conditions within the prison. In the 1770s, the prison reformer John Howard visited Newgate and was appalled to find that nearly 150 women were crowded into three or four rooms, with similar issues on the men's side, which included boys of 12 or 14, some of whom were nearly naked. However, as the 19th century progressed, the situation in Newgate improved. The work of reformers, such as Elizabeth Fry, and the construction of new detention prisons within London, led to dramatic changes in the way the prisoners were treated in Newgate, as well as a gradual decrease in the numbers incarcerated there. The latter figure was most impacted by the opening of new prisons for London: Pentonville in 1842 and Holloway in 1849. The opening of Holloway, in particular, saw Newgate become mainly a holding prison for those awaiting trial or execution.

THE CONDEMNED CELL

The arrangements for holding the condemned at Newgate while they awaited execution varied over time. In the earlier prison the condemned hold was a single cell in which numerous people could be held. By 1726, construction was started on separate

'Incredible scenes of horror occur in Newgate.'

Edward Gibbon Wakefield, politician, 1831

↑ *Waist restraints with handcuffs, Newgate Prison, 19th century.*
The handcuffs attached to the waist restraint forced the prisoner to keep their arms by their sides.

cells for the condemned and in Dance's prison of 1782, the cells for the condemned resembled stone dungeons, each with a small, high window. A description of Newgate in 1810 describes fifteen condemned cells, ten for male prisoners and five for female ones, arranged over three floors adjacent to the Press Yard. There was also a day room for the use of the condemned. At this time the condemned cells would usually hold two or three prisoners, although sometimes more. During the 1830s, the condemned cells were enlarged by knocking two rooms into one, in part reflecting the decline in death sentences. The cell blocks at Newgate were rebuilt in 1859–61 in a bid to modernise them, and the new block included only two condemned cells, each to house a single prisoner.

Until the early 19th century, the condemned had to wear iron waist belts, often attached to leg irons, which forced prisoners to stoop forward when attempting to walk. Sometimes prisoners were allowed padding to stop the irons cutting into their legs. *The Statesman* newspaper, reporting on the execution of Thomas Bedworth in 1815, noted: 'When he was introduced into the Press-yard, he requested Davis to give the leggings (pieces of leather to prevent the irons from excoriating the flesh) to a prisoner who had been very serviceable to him on many occasions.' Many of the condemned had handcuffs as well as leg irons. Loaded with heavy chains, they could barely walk, the sound of their every movement reverberating throughout the prison. The practice of routinely keeping prisoners shackled in irons ceased in the 1820s.

Newgate was notorious for corruption and abuse. Alcohol and other substances were readily available for a price, and many of the condemned went to the gallows intoxicated. Others, although watched constantly, attempted to take their own lives by ingesting smuggled poison. In December 1829 a phial of prussic acid poison, often taken by prisoners to avoid the trauma of the gallows, was found in the condemned cell

↑ *The condemned cell, Newgate, 1878.*
The single small, high window allows only limited light into the sparse cell. By this time public executions had ended and Newgate held far fewer prisoners.
PUBLISHED IN THE ILLUSTRATED LONDON NEWS, 29 DECEMBER 1888.

PRISON REFORMER

Elizabeth Fry (1780–1845)

The prison reformer Elizabeth Fry was a regular visitor to Newgate's female prisoners. Born into a well-to-do Quaker family in Norwich, she settled in London after her marriage to Joseph Fry. The Frys had eleven children. Fry had a strong social conscience and, in 1813, through a family friend, she visited Newgate Prison for the first time. She was horrified by the squalor she found there, particularly among the women and children (during this period, Newgate both held child prisoners and was home to the children of prisoners). In 1817, she was deeply affected by her visits to a female prisoner awaiting execution. She wrote in her journal: 'This has been a time of deep humiliation to me, this witnessing the effect of the consequences of sin. The poor creature murdered her baby; and how inexpressibly awful now to have her life taken away.'

Fry ensured that a school was opened in Newgate and a matron was appointed to stay at the prison and supervise the women prisoners and their care. Fry and her associates sought to bring both moral and religious support to the women, including those awaiting execution. She instigated a scheme that subdivided the female prisoners into smaller groups for instruction. They were taught sewing and reading; the sewing resulted in the production of clothing for export to the Australian penal colony. In 1821, she formed the British Ladies' Society for Promoting the Reformation of Female Prisoners. She travelled widely, visiting prisons and meeting heads of state and gave evidence to parliamentary committees. Her work in raising awareness of appalling prison conditions was influential in the passing of the Gaols Act 1823, which included reforms such as the segregation of male and female prisoners and the appointment of female warders for female prisoners. Many Quakers spoke out publicly against capital punishment, believing it conflicted with their religion. Although Fry comforted the condemned, she never openly campaigned for the total abolition of the death penalty.

Admit the Bearer to the Female Side of Newgate, at half-past Ten on the Instant.

← *Elizabeth Fry's Newgate Prison Pass, c.1815–20.*

↑ *Newgate Prison key, 1830.* The key was gifted to Elizabeth Fry by the Chief Warder of Newgate in recognition of her work among the prisoners.

↑ *Elizabeth Fry's bonnet, c.1840.*
Quaker bonnets, with their lack of
decoration and deep brims, became
the most recognisable component of
female Quaker dress.

← *Elizabeth Fry (detail), c.1823.*
She wears a muslin Quaker cap
similar to that shown below.
OIL ON PANEL, AFTER CHARLES ROBERT LESLIE.

← *Muslin Quaker Cap worn
by Elizabeth Fry, c.1840.*
Fry was often depicted undertaking
her prison work wearing a simple
muslin cap. Followers of the Quaker
religion traditionally wore plain
clothing in muted colours. She
reflected: 'I used to think and do
now how little dress matters. But I
find it almost impossible to keep to
the principles of Friends without
altering my dress and speech [...] They
appear to me a sort of protector to
the principles of Christianity in the
present state of the world.'

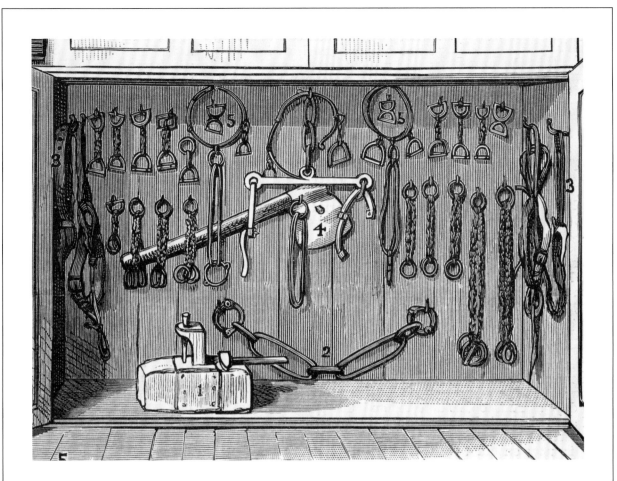

that was being shared by four men. One of the men, 24-year-old Stephan Sandford, wrote to the Governor giving the names of two suppliers of prussic acid within Newgate. The letter indicates the ease with which prisoners could obtain the poison that caused instant death. Sandford's motives for revealing the names on the eve of his execution are unclear but his letter did not spare him the gallows. The previous year Captain John Burgh Montgomery succeeded in taking his own life. He was aged about 39 and had been found guilty of forging banknotes. The morning after he wrote his last letter, he was found dead on his bed beside a phial of poison.

Condemned prisoners exercised in the Press Yard at Newgate and, from the 1820s, when conditions improved, they could talk to visitors through a double grating near the yard gate. When prison inspectors visited Newgate in 1836, they reported that the condemned received extra diet, as did those who were sick or 'suckling'. During the 19th century, as attitudes changed, the

↑ *The Chain Cupboard, Newgate Prison,* **Illustrated London News,** *December 29, 1888.*
This illustration accompanied an article about the future demolition of Newgate. The Chain Cupboard is described as holding both modern items that are still in use and older pieces such as 'Chains from which John 'Jack' Sheppard freed himself' and 'Axe, formerly carried before Prisoners at Executions, another version being that it was made for the Cato Street Conspirators [of 1820] but not used'.

situation for the condemned changed too. The majority expected and received a reprieve from execution. Visiting the prison in the 1830s, Charles Dickens observed 25 condemned prisoners in the day room who, in anticipation of a reprieve, showed 'very little anxiety or mental suffering'.

LAST LETTERS AND MEMENTOES

The condemned traditionally composed last letters and final requests on the eve of their execution. Addressed to the Prison Governor or Ordinary, they often included messages for loved ones, declarations of innocence and repentance, or requests for last visits and alcohol. Many were very personal. The Museum of London holds a number of letters dating from the 1820s and 1830s. All are addressed either to the Keeper (Governor) of Newgate, John Wontner, or to the Ordinary, the Reverend Dr Horace Cotton. Interestingly a number of the letters appear to be handwritten by the condemned, confirming their literacy.

Rarer survivals are mementoes left by the condemned. Having few possessions remaining with them, they had little to pass to their loved ones as a keepsake of them. Some condemned

← *Henry Jubilee Conway, aged 19, executed at Newgate for forgery, 27 July 1829.*
Conway's letter lists the relatives and friends, including his wife, to whom he wishes to say goodbye. It also declares his 'true repentance'. Conway and an accomplice were accused of forging cheques and trying to cash them; he was found guilty of one charge. His wife had given birth to a son, their first child, only five weeks before his execution.

prisoners engraved smoothed coins with illustrations and messages. These were known as Newgate tokens or leaden hearts. A visitor in the 1830s recorded seeing inmates 'grinding the impressions off penny-pieces, then pricking figures or words on them to give to their friends as memorials.' The two illustrated here both show execution scenes and were, presumably, made by or for those in the condemned cells.

←↑ Convict tokens, 1755–80. One token (top) is made from a copper halfpenny, with decoration scratched into its surfaces. One side shows a body hanging from a gallows, and on the reverse is a double gallows with two bodies hanging from it. The other token (left) shows a woman hanging from a gallows, while on the other side, which is now almost illegible, a house with a tree is depicted.

CELEBRITY CRIMINAL PORTRAITS

Portraits increasingly accompanied accounts of high-profile crimes in the popular press from the 17th century. These were usually quite crude and generic depictions. Some offenders, however, were of such interest to the public that enterprising artists paid the gaolers to gain access in order to draw accurate likenesses. By charging artists, biographers, journalists and even curious individuals for visits, sittings and interviews, the condemned could buy small luxuries and potentially even gain some control over their public image.

FINAL CLOTHING

Many condemned criminals thought very carefully about what they would wear for their last moments. There was a theatrical aspect to the staging of public executions and the majority of prisoners were aware that all eyes would be on them. In 1587, at her execution in Fotherhay Castle in Northamptonshire, Mary, Queen of Scots wore a black gown, which was removed on the scaffold to reveal a red-brown gown, red being the colour of martyrdom. John Bradford, the Protestant preacher, demonstrated his piety by wearing a white 'shirt of flame' which had been specially made for him for his execution in 1555. The shirt was compared to 'a wedding garment', signifying and celebrating his readiness to die for his faith.

Details of the clothing worn by the condemned were often noted in the press descriptions of executions, particularly when the condemned was a woman and, even more so, a young woman.

THE IRISH LAUNDRESS

Sarah Malcolm, aged 22, executed on 7 March 1733

← Sarah Malcolm (detail), 1733.

Hogarth painted this portrait from sketches he made of Malcolm in her cell, two days before her execution. The writer and politician Horace Walpole bought the painting from Hogarth.

OIL ON CANVAS BY WILLIAM HOGARTH.

← Sarah Malcolm (detail), 1733.

One of several prints based on the painting of Malcolm by Hogarth, this example adds two salacious extra details: the scene of her execution and the figure of a clergyman holding a ring. The latter is thought by some to be Revd W. Piddington, who published Malcolm's biography and with whom she was rumoured to have had a romantic relationship.

ETCHING, AFTER WILLIAM HOGARTH, C.1733.

Sarah Malcolm, known as the 'Irish Laundress' because her mother was Irish, was born in Durham and moved to London with her parents. She was educated and could read and write, but her family had fallen on hard times. She became laundress to a number of people who rented rooms in the Temple Chambers. In 1733, she was convicted of involvement in the robbery and murder of three women there. Her trial at the Old Bailey lasted about five hours, during which she spoke eloquently and cross-examined a number of witnesses for half an hour in her defence. Unusually for the time she spoke openly about her menstruation, claiming the blood on her clothing was not from the murders but due to her period, and she questioned the witnesses closely about whether the blood was wet or dry and exactly where on her clothing they had seen it. The trial was sensationally reported and many writers visited her in Newgate, hoping to publish her story. Leading painter William Hogarth also came to sketch her portrait, visiting with his father-in-law, the painter Sir James Thornhill. Their visit took place just days before her execution and was reported in the newspapers of the day.

Malcolm admitted the burglary but maintained her innocence of murder until the end and was hanged on Fleet Street within sight of Temple Chambers, in front of a vast crowd. This public interest in her created a healthy market for prints of William Hogarth's portrait.

Prison reformer Elizabeth Fry wrote that the 'chief thought' of most condemned women at Newgate was 'the dress in which she shall be hanged'. In 1733, the press reports of the execution of Sarah Malcolm noted: 'She was dressed in a black Gown, white Apron, Sarsenet [a soft silk] Hood, and black Gloves.' When Eliza Fenning was hanged in 1815 for attempting to poison her employers, she wore 'a white muslin gown, a handsome worked cap and laced boots'. Wearing white might have emphasised her claim of innocence, but white muslin gowns were also highly fashionable at this time. The public was greatly moved by her case and rumours circulated that Fenning was hanged in the

> *'Her dress was pure white. The most heart-rending sensations pervaded the minds of the thousands who witnessed the dreadful scene.'*
>
> Jackson's Oxford Journal, describing Eliza Fenning, 29 July 1815

dress she had intended to wear to her wedding. At her funeral, the pall – the cloth that covered the coffin – was attended by six young women also wearing white.

Laurence Shirley, Earl Ferrers, was hanged on 5 May 1760 for the murder of his steward John Johnson, whom he shot in a rage. His execution was unusual for a number of reasons, not least that Ferrers travelled from the Tower in his own carriage

↑ *The execution of Earl Ferrers, 5 May 1760.*
ENGRAVING, C.1760.

with a series of coaches and guards, contrasting with the usual procession of carts from Newgate. Particular note was made about his clothing, which was described variously as 'a superb suit of white and silver, being the clothes in which he was married' and a 'light coloured coat and sattin [sic] waistcoat, embroidered with silver; and black breeches'. These had been his wedding clothes and, according to Lord Orford, Ferrers 'thought this, at least, as good an occasion for putting them on, as that for which they were first made'. Ferrers's reason was that 'they had been his first step towards ruin and should attend his exit'. His wife Mary had formally separated from him on account of his cruelty.

Once an execution had been completed, the executioner was allowed to keep the clothing of the executed as part of their fee. Hannah Dagoe, executed for robbery in 1763, either threw some of her clothes into the crowd or gave them to an acquaintance, in order to prevent this, notwithstanding some struggles from the hangman to retain them. Newspapers describe her 'dressed very clean, in a silk bonnet, cardinal [a hooded cloak] and mourning gown'. She was executed alongside Paul Lewis, a highwayman, who 'was dressed in a white cloth Coat, blue silk waistcoat trimmed with silver, a silver-laced hat, white stockings and silk breeches'. Sometimes individuals wore their shroud – the often plain, white garment in which they would be buried – to their execution. Stephen Gardener, executed for housebreaking in February 1724, wore only a shroud, despite the cold, to show regret for his sins; similarly, in 1743, Andrew Millar travelled to his execution at Execution Dock in a cart together with his coffin and wearing his shroud.

RELIGION AND REPENTANCE

Religion played a central role in prisoners' lives, especially for those awaiting a death sentence. They were visited regularly by the Newgate Prison chaplain, the Ordinary, and at the daily chapel services they sat in the 'condemned pew' facing him. The Ordinary's Account, a record kept of the chaplain's visits to the condemned, shows that, alongside spiritual comfort and consolation, the Ordinary also made strenuous efforts to persuade the unrepentant to repent. Although prisoners were urged to subscribe to Church of England practices, provision was made for those who maintained other faiths. Catholic priests, Methodist ministers, rabbis and imams called on

'...the Ordinary and his assistants [...] almost live with the condemned men, exhorting them to repentance, prayer and faith.'
Edward Gibbon Wakefield, politician, 1831

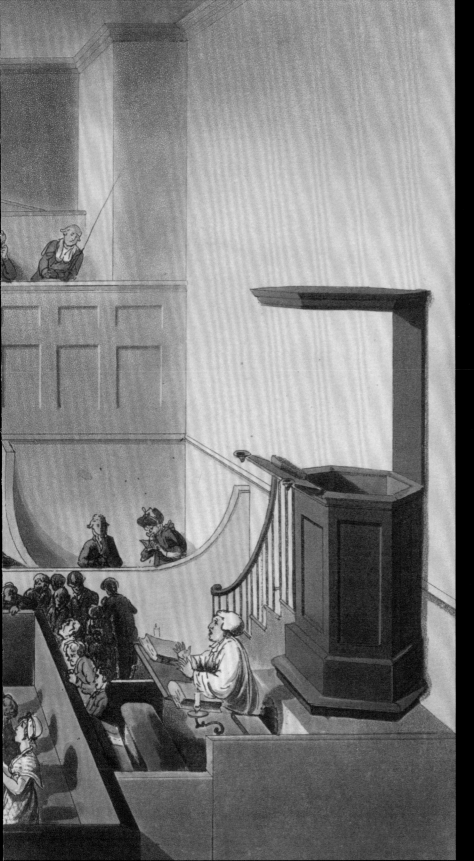

← **The Condemned Sermon, Newgate Prison, 1809.**

On the Sunday before their death, the condemned would attend Newgate Chapel for their 'last sermon'. They were made to sit around a coffin placed in an enclosure called the Dock.

ETCHING BY CHARLES PUGIN AND THOMAS ROWLANDSON WITH AQUATINT BY JOSEPH CONSTANTINE STADLER, PUBLISHED BY RUDOLPH ACKERMANN, 1809.

prisoners and sometimes accompanied them to the scaffold. In 1743, Abraham Pass, a Jew from Bordeaux, was allowed 'Jewish Priests or Rabbis' to comfort him and pray with him before his execution for the theft of some linen cloth from a house. Similarly, in 1771, a rabbi visited Levi Weil and his Jewish gang of robbers, providing them with Hebrew texts. He did not accompany them to their execution, however, because they had been cast out from the synagogue after their conviction of robbing a widow, Mrs Hutchings, in Chelsea and murdering one of her farm labourers. In 1814, Munoo, a Lascar sailor, aged 28 and described as being from the East Indies, was executed for committing an 'unnatural offence' on an eight-year-old boy in a field near Shadwell. The press of the time mentioned that he was Muslim and that he was visited by an imam called Mauljee and his attendant, both the night before and on the morning of his execution. Mr Gould, the superintendent of the Lascars, was also allowed to be with him on the morning of his execution.

On the Sunday before their execution, condemned prisoners in Newgate heard the 'condemned sermon', which was preached by the Ordinary. The subject preached in the sermon, and the verses read and the hymns sung in the remainder of the service, were selected to be appropriate as a final lesson for those preparing to die. Their emotion – terror, despair or feigned nonchalance – was witnessed by other prisoners and members of the public, who could pay an entrance fee to attend the service and hear the 'condemned sermon'. This practice of selling tickets continued until the early 19th century, when it was banned on grounds of taste. However, the authorities relented in 1840 and sold tickets for the 'condemned sermon' of François Courvoisier, the Swiss valet who was convicted of murdering his master, in response to the enormous public interest in the case.

↑ An execution broadside from 1814.
This execution broadside mentions the indictment of a Lascar sailor called Munoo for an 'unnatural offence'. He was executed at Newgate on 23 December 1814, aged 28.

CHAPTER 4

THE DAY OF EXECUTION

The rituals and ceremony of execution days were deeply etched into the culture of London life. The crowd, the condemned, the hangman and religious and civic officials all played a role in the spectacle. The state regarded execution days as a public demonstration of its power over the life and death of its citizens. Freed from their leg irons, the condemned prepared to face the audience awaiting their entrance onto London's most dramatic public stage. Although choreographed to deter others from falling into a life of crime, execution day could result in public disorder, proclamations of innocence, and bungled executions.

From 1783 until 1868, when public execution was abolished, most executions took place just outside Newgate Prison. This meant that the condemned were no longer forced to make the journey from Newgate in the City of London to Tyburn in the west, which had become an important part of the ritual of execution day. Whether at Tyburn or Newgate or elsewhere in London, the moment of death evoked conflicting emotions within the crowd, from irreverent mocking to respectful silence.

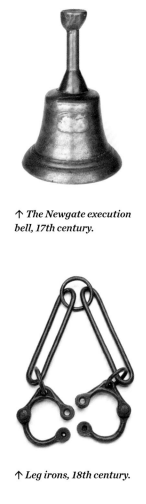

↑ *The Newgate execution bell, 17th century.*

↑ *Leg irons, 18th century.*

THE MORNING OF THE EXECUTION

At midnight on the night before executions, the bell-man, or church clerk, from Holy Sepulchre Church (also known as St Sepulchre-without-Newgate) would ring a handbell, known as the execution bell, twelve times outside the condemned cell in Newgate Prison. He would recite a verse encouraging the prisoners to repent of their sins:

> *All you that in the condemned hole do lie,*
> *Prepare you, for tomorrow you shall die,*
> *Watch all, and pray: the hour is drawing near*
> *That you before the Almighty must appear.*
> *Examine well yourselves, in time repent,*
> *That you may not to eternal flames be sent,*
> *And when St Sepulchre's Bell in the morning tolls,*
> *The Lord above have mercy on your souls.*

Robert Dowe began this custom through a bequest of £50 to the church in 1605, for them to buy a handbell to mark the executions of prisoners held in Newgate. The tradition ended in the early 19th century. As the Newgate bell rang for the condemned at midnight, Londoners began to gather at the execution site.

On the morning of execution day, those condemned who were deemed worthy and appropriately repentant, with the exception of murderers, received Communion.

The final ritual to take place within the prison was for the condemned to have their leg irons removed by a blacksmith in Newgate's Press Yard or later in the Upper Condemned Cell, a large room in the upper part of the prison. Their hands were then secured, and their 'halter' (noose) tied around their waists. They were then ready to leave the prison.

> *'All the way from Newgate to Tyburn, is one continued fair, for whores and rogues of the meaner sort. It is incredible what a scene of confusion all this often makes...'*
> Bernard Mandeville, philosopher, 1725

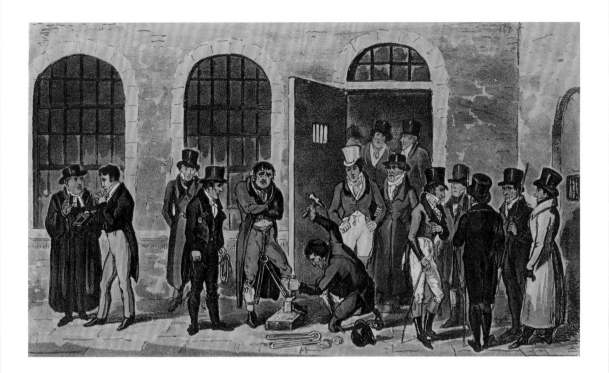

PROCESSION TO TYBURN

The procession to the gallows was a 4.5-kilometre journey from Newgate Prison via Holborn, St Giles and Tyburn Road (modern Oxford Street), but it could take up to three hours. It took place eight times a year and constituted London's most regular and well-attended pageant. The condemned were carried in open carts – often sitting on their own coffins. They rode with their backs to the horses, facing the crowd, and were accompanied by the hangman and the Ordinary of Newgate. The cavalcade was led by the City Marshal and guarded by cavalry and soldiers or 'javelin' men, since the procession to an execution was risky: there was always a chance that someone might attempt to rescue the prisoners on the way. This happened in 1351, but the condemned man was later recaptured and hanged. The 'javelin' men carried halberds and other staff weapons as they marched alongside the prisoners to prevent such interference. Even when executions moved to Newgate, the City Marshal and his marshalmen attended to ensure that order was maintained. The tipstaves, or short decorated clubs, that they carried were symbols of their authority but also could be used as weapons.

The first ritual to be carried out on the procession to Tyburn took place shortly after the cart had left Newgate. As it arrived at

↑ Removing a condemned prisoner's leg irons in the Press Yard at Newgate, 1821.

This scene from Pierce Egan's serialised fiction *Life in London*, shows a condemned prisoner having his leg irons removed. The yeoman of the halter stands next to him. Further left is the Ordinary of Newgate, praying with another prisoner. In the centre, in front of the door, stand three gentlemen visitors who have come to witness this 'afflicting scene', one of whom talks to the group of sheriffs to the right.

ENGRAVING BY ISAAC RICHARD AND GEORGE CRUIKSHANK, 1821.

FAUNTLEROY'S LAST HOURS

In 1824, the banker Henry Fauntleroy was found guilty of forgery and embezzlement, and was sentenced to death. A partner in a Marylebone banking firm, he forged his clients' signatures to embezzle funds which he used to finance extramarital affairs. The scandal of his crime attracted considerable public attention in the popular press, much of it favourable to his case. Despite seventeen respectable character witnesses at his trial, two appeals and a petition of 13,000 names, his conviction was not overturned. It was reported that 100,000 people attended his execution at Newgate on 30 November 1824. He was one of the last people to be executed for forgery, the final person being Thomas Maynard at Newgate in 1829. The death penalty was abolished for all forms of forgery by the Forgery Act 1837.

↓ *The Upper Condemned Cell at Newgate Prison on the morning of the execution of Henry Fauntleroy, 1824.*
This painting depicts Henry Fauntleroy on the morning of his execution, 30 November 1824. This is not one of the normal condemned cells at Newgate, but the Upper Condemned Cell, a large room on the upper floor to which prisoners were brought on the morning of their execution. Fauntleroy, due to his wealthy background, was treated as a special case and had stayed in the chamber of one of the warders, rather than a cell. Fauntleroy stands in a dark suit, slightly to the left of centre. The executioner, wearing a pale shirt and waistcoat, secures Fauntleroy's arms from

behind. The turnkey (jailor) Harris stands behind them in a brown coat. The group of men standing to the left includes the Reverend Dr Horace Cotton, Ordinary of Newgate, with grey hair, dressed in his robes. He would accompany the condemned to the scaffold. To the right of Fauntleroy, a blacksmith removes the leg irons from another prisoner. Fauntleroy was executed alone, so this man is either having his shackles removed for a different reason or is an invented character. On the right of the picture, a sheriff of the City of London stands with another prisoner, whose arms and hands have been tied so that he cannot escape but can still pray.

OIL ON CANVAS BY WILLIAM THOMSON, 1828.

the wall of Holy Sepulchre Church, the bell-man rang the same handbell that the condemned had heard at midnight, and read a further prayer warning the condemned of their need to repent and asking those present to pray for their souls. Until the end of the 18th century, the condemned were also presented with a nosegay, a small bunch of flowers, at the steps of the church.

The rest of the journey was often a boisterous affair, with lively crowds lining the route, cheering or jeering as the condemned passed by. But when Dr Archibald Cameron of Lochiel was drawn on a sledge to Tyburn from the Tower of London, the onlookers stood still and watched respectfully. According to the *Newgate Calendar*, they 'all pitied his situation'. Sometimes individual characters in the crowd became famous, such as John Gale. He became a notorious London figure associated with the Tyburn processions around the turn of the 18th century. Known as Dumb Jack, because he was deaf and mute, 'his greatest mental enjoyment' according to his biographers, was 'that of witnessing the public execution of criminals, whom he constantly accompanied from the gaol to Tyburn, riding on the [...] cart'. Another tradition that formed part of the Tyburn journey was stopping for refreshments – usually gin – at inns at St Giles-in-the-Fields, and at the Mason's Arms, Seymour Place. Most of those who stopped at the Mason's Arms would have known that the Tyburn scaffold was only minutes away.

TYBURN'S 'TRIPLE TREE' GALLOWS

There had been executions at Tyburn since the end of the 12th century. In the earliest days, people were probably hanged from trees. In 1571, a 'new pair of gallows made in triangular manner' was erected. This had three wooden crossbeams, each with space to hang eight people, allowing up to 24 criminals to be hanged at once. This 'Triple Tree' permanent gallows was taken down in 1759 and a movable gallows that could be brought out just on execution days was used instead until 1783, when hangings moved to Newgate.

The gallows was located at Tyburn because it was one of the major roads in and out of London. However, by the mid 18th century, traffic had increased and the construction in 1761 of a hexagonal toll house close to the site of the gallows added to the congestion. Here, people using the turnpike would have to stop to pay the toll. Execution days caused huge disruption to traffic along the turnpike. Locals complained about the inconvenience and started campaigning to have the execution site relocated.

↑ *Dr Archibald Cameron being drawn on a sledge to Tyburn, 7 June 1753.*
Dr Archibald Cameron of Lochiel was the last of the Scottish Jacobite rebels to be executed for high treason. He was drawn on a sledge from the Tower of London to Tyburn, before being hanged until he was dead. His heart was then taken out and burned.
ENGRAVING, PUBLISHED IN THE NEWGATE CALENDAR, 1795.

By the mid 18th century, the area around Tyburn was also becoming gentrified. In 1768–9 a petition from 125 Tyburn residents was sent to the Lord Mayor of London. The residents complained that they could not get in or out of their homes on execution days on account of the 'vast concourse of people' and 'great tumults, disturbances, riots and nuisances' that occurred. They stated that horses and carriages could not pass on the roads without 'the greatest difficulty and danger'. An attached plan suggested an alternative gallows site in Camden. The petition was unsuccessful but eventually the execution site was moved to Newgate.

NEWGATE EXECUTIONS

From 1783, when executions ceased at Tyburn, until 1868, criminals condemned at the Old Bailey were executed in front of the newly rebuilt Newgate Prison. The demolition of buildings in front of the rebuilt prison provided a new space for public execution. Its central position enabled the authorities to reinstate their command of the crowd. The forbidding prison provided an imposing backdrop to the spectacle. Without the lengthy – and potentially unruly – procession, and with the mechanised 'new

drop' system of hanging, the authorities hoped to orchestrate a more regulated execution process. This was supposed to enable better control of the crowd, concentrating their attention on the moral message of the gallows.

As before, prior to leaving Newgate for the scaffold, the arms and hands of prisoners were restrained to prevent resistance. However, from the mid 19th century, arms were pinioned by a leather body belt. This replaced the use of cord that allowed the prisoner to pray but could also result in an undignified struggle when the time of execution came.

Prisoners passed through three doors at Newgate Prison on their way to the scaffold. As the bolt was drawn on the Debtors' Door, the third and final door they would go through, the condemned would become aware of the massive crowd awaiting their appearance and would prepare to take their last steps before being 'launched into eternity'. The new mechanised gallows outside Newgate was seen as a model of efficiency and modernity. The executioner only had to pull a lever and a trapdoor would drop, hanging 'ten malefactors' at once. The

↑ *The new gallows at Newgate, 1783.*
ENGRAVING BY WILLIAM GRAINGER, PUBLISHED BY ALEXANDER HOGG, C.1826.

↓ *Leather pinioning belt, c.1850–99.*

attention of every spectator would be focused on the stagelike scaffold. The gallows became known as the 'sheriff's picture frame' in this period, suggesting the sense of public execution as a moralising display.

LAST RITES

Whether at Tyburn or Newgate, Horsemonger Lane or Execution Dock, the final moments of the condemned followed a set pattern. When they arrived at the gallows, the prisoners might make a speech, pass money to the hangman, sing hymns and say some final prayers. For those travelling to Tyburn, the noose had usually already been placed around their neck while in the Press Yard at Newgate, with the slack wound round their waist, restraining them during their journey to the gallows. Once there, the hangman and his assistant would throw the slack over the gallows, or later, guide the condemned to the right location on the trapdoor. The condemned would be blindfolded or have a hood placed over their head, if they had brought one with them. The hood was originally a plain white nightcap of the type commonly worn by many Londoners in bed. In July 1780, when William Pateman was about to be hanged on Coleman Street for his part in the Gordon Riots, he was asked for his cap, but said he had forgotten to bring it with him. A cap was sourced from a house opposite, and the execution went ahead. A plain white hood later became a standard part of the execution paraphernalia brought to the scaffold for those that wanted it.

THE CROWD

Tens of thousands of spectators attended the executions of high-profile or notorious criminals. It was estimated that 30,000 people watched the unusual hanging in 1776 of twin brothers Daniel and Robert Perreau, for forgery. But the press of people, often funnelled through relatively narrow spaces, or packed onto temporary wooden stands, meant that there was little the authorities could do to control the crowd. The risk of public disorder or disaster was ever present. When a surge in 1807 led to the deaths of about 30 people, the crowd was estimated at about 40,000. But for the most famous criminals, such as John 'Jack' Sheppard, crowds of 100,000 or even 200,000 were estimated to have turned out. At Tyburn, special stands were erected

↑ *Newgate Prison Debtors' Door, c.1780.*
This was the third and final door condemned prisoners passed through on their way to the scaffold. It was in use from the first public execution outside Newgate in 1783 until the last in 1868. It was originally installed as the entrance to the debtors' prison.

THE CATO STREET CONSPIRACY

One of the most notorious executions outside Newgate Prison was that of the five leaders of the Cato Street Conspiracy in 1820. The men had plotted to overthrow the government by assassinating the Prime Minister, Lord Liverpool, together with his cabinet. They wanted to start a radical revolution and to set up their own provisional government, but were betrayed by a government spy. Arthur Thistlewood, Richard Tidd, James Ings, William Davidson and John Brunt were charged with conspiracy to subvert the constitution and to levy war: treasonable offences for which the sentence was drawing, hanging and quartering. The public's appetite for written and graphic representations of the arrest, trial and execution of the accused was insatiable. A sketch by the leading French history painter Théodore Géricault is thought to have been made at the execution. Newspapers reported that many present expressed sympathy for the condemned and booed the executioner. Fearing violent disorder, the government stationed soldiers and artillery around the area to keep the peace.

← *Axe made for the execution of the Cato Street conspirators, 1820.*

This axe was not used to behead the men but was placed on the scaffold near the wooden block on which the men's heads were severed by a masked man with a surgical knife, after they had died on the gallows. It is likely that this is the axe illustrated in the image of the Chain Cupboard at Newgate from 1888 (page 66).

← *William Davidson, one of the Cato Street conspirators, 1820.*

William Davidson was the son of the attorney general of Jamaica and a local African woman. He studied law and mathematics in Scotland, spent time at sea and worked as a cabinet maker in Birmingham and London. Following the massacre of protesters at St Peter's Fields, Manchester, in 1819, he became involved in radical politics. He joined the organising committee of the Cato Street Conspiracy and was one of the five to be executed.

ENGRAVING BY ROBERT COOPER AFTER ABRAHAM WIVELL IN GEORGE THEODORE WILKINSON, AN AUTHENTIC HISTORY OF THE CATO-STREET CONSPIRACY, 1820.

THE TRUE MANER OF THE EXECUTION OF THOMAS EARLE OF STRAFFORD. LORD
Lieutenant of Ireland vpon Tower hill the 12ᵗ of May 1641.

HYBERNIÆ PROREGIS SUPPLICIVM ·

A. Doctor Vsher, Lord Prima-
ie of Ireland.
B. the Sherifes of London
C. the Earle of Strafford.
D. his kindred and friends.

Execution des Grafen Thomæ von Stafford Statthalter in Jrland auf de Tawers platz in Londen 12 Maj 1641.

A. Doct. Ulher Primat in Irland.   C. Der Graf von Stafford.
B. Rahts Herren von London.   D. Seine anverwänten vnd freunde.

for execution days. The wealthy could book a seat in 'Mother Proctor's pews' to get a good look at the execution scene. When executions moved from Tyburn and began to be performed outside Newgate Prison, a space on a rooftop, or a window in the upper storeys of one of the surrounding houses could be hired to give the best views. Most people, however, joined the general throng that surrounded the gallows, often spreading out into surrounding streets.

People's reasons for watching varied. Some wanted to see justice done but there was always a fascination with death. The 18th-century lawyer James Boswell confessed, 'I feel an irresistible impulse to be present at every execution.' The crowd's reaction was also mixed. They booed the hangman if they sympathised with the condemned but murderers were generally met with insults and catcalls.

It could be dangerous to attend an execution. Pickpockets were a constant hazard and there were many instances of shoddily made stands collapsing, leading to deaths and injuries.

↑ *Execution of Thomas Wentworth, Earl of Strafford, 12 May 1641.*
The beheading of Wentworth, a supporter of King Charles I, on Tower Hill was witnessed by a crowd of thousands. Wenceslaus Hollar's etching of the event includes people attempting to climb onto makeshift platforms, while on the left an over-full stand collapses.
ETCHING BY WENCESLAUS HOLLAR, 1641.

The worst incident was on 23 February 1807, when a huge crowd attended a triple execution. The crowd tripped over a pieman's stand and, as the 'multitude' surged from adjoining streets, a wagon also overturned, trampling and crushing the fallen. In the region of 30 people were killed, three of them female. By far the majority were young men aged between ten and twenty, including six apprentices. Of the three women, one had brought with her 'a child at the breast'. The baby survived, according to *The Times*, by being thrown from one person to another and finally placed under a cart until the crush was over. Twenty years later, in 1827, a temporary seating stand collapsed during the execution of Mary Wittenback. She had been convicted of the murder of her husband by 'administering arsenic' in his pudding and her execution was attended by many women. When the stand collapsed, eleven people were thrown into the crowd, many of whom were saved by being hoisted through the window of an adjoining house. At Execution Dock, it was not unknown for spectators to fall into the river and drown while watching an execution.

THE EXECUTION ECONOMY

Attended by crowds of tens of thousands, public execution had a significant impact on London's economy. The long wait at the gallows proved highly lucrative for street sellers of 'gallows literature' and refreshments. The hire of window views and grandstand seating to wealthier spectators benefited both individual householders and the authorities. Pickpockets profited from the crush, while the holiday atmosphere benefitted taverns, alehouses and prostitutes. Critics argued that public execution days disrupted London's economy and encouraged idleness and the loss of working hours.

Gallows literature

Prior to the emergence of national newspapers, unofficial and often sensationalist accounts of crimes and executions were published in cheap pamphlets and broadsides. These were sold by patterers at the site of execution and, in the following days, throughout the country. A 'good murder' could sell up to 250,000 copies. Written in the language of the street and quickly printed in advance they often mistakenly described the execution of reprieved prisoners. Printers used the same wooden printing

'Several of the nobility, and other persons of distinction, saw the execution from the neighbouring houses; and there was as great a concourse of common people as ever was on the like occasion. Many of the spectators were hurt by the breaking down of a scaffold; and a great many ladies and gentlemen had their pockets pick'd or cut off.'

Derby Mercury, 15 March 1733, describing the execution of Sarah Malcolm at Mitre Court, Fleet Street

'A hanging day was to all intents and purposes a fair day.'

Francis Place, social reformer, c.1828

THE TYBURN CROWD

One of the best depictions of an execution crowd and the attendant, almost carnival, atmosphere, is this engraving by William Hogarth from 1747. It comes from a set of twelve prints by Hogarth comparing the virtue of 'Industry' and the vice of 'Idleness'. Two apprentices, the hard-working and honest Francis Goodchild and the lazy Tom Idle, are given the same chances in life, but the first makes the most of them and rises to be Lord Mayor of London, while the other squanders them and sinks into criminality. This scene shows the final part of the procession towards the Tyburn gallows.

To the left of centre, Tom Idle sits in a cart with his own coffin on the way to the gallows while a Methodist minister exhorts him to repentance. Ahead of them, the hangman nonchalantly smokes his pipe while awaiting the condemned, lying on top of Tyburn's famous Triple Tree gallows. Meanwhile, in the centre of the image, a fight breaks out in the crowd between street sellers. Next to them, a broadside seller hawks copies of 'The Last dying speech & confession of Tho Idle', even though he has not yet given a speech. And to the right, a boy pickpockets the gingerbread seller known as Tiddy Doll, while spectators clamber up onto a cart to get a better view and others get drunk.

↑ *The Idle 'Prentice Executed at Tyburn, 1747.*
ENGRAVING BY WILLIAM HOGARTH, 1747.

12 Months in London

← *A London patterer, or street seller, 1798.*
Sorrowful last dying speeches and confessions of the condemned were recited at the site of execution by street sellers. Printed versions were sold to the crowd. Often scripted by the printers and sellers themselves, the same dying speeches were used multiple times, with a few minor changes and usually included a moral message of repentance.
WATERCOLOUR BY THOMAS ROWLANDSON, 1798.

block for the gallows scene but changed the number of hanging figures as required. The block used for women was cut square at the knee to represent a skirt. The broadsides usually gave details of the last speeches made on the scaffold and recounted how the execution had gone. Often the speeches and descriptions were generic, reused again and again with little adaptation, for a rapacious and eager audience. The broadsides were primarily published by a small number of printers such as Thomas Birt, James Catnach and James Pitts, located in the Seven Dials area of London. Broadsides sometimes featured ballads and songs commemorating the executed and their crimes. The story would be written in verse that was then set to recognisable tunes.

→ *'The Dreadful Murder of Mrs Crouch, at Marylebone', 1844.*
This ballad describing the murder of Frances Crouch by her husband, William, was published by Thomas Birt. William Crouch was hanged at Newgate on 27 May 1844.

COPY OF VERSES

On the Dreadful Murder of Mrs. CROUCH, at Marylebone

Oh, a dreadful tale I will unfold,
  Occurred on Saturday night,
When William Crouch as it appears
  Did slay his lawful wife ;
Number 4, in Little Marylebone-street,
  He in a rage did go,
Which has filled the neighbourhood
  With sorrow, grief, and woe.

It was on March the thirtieth,
  Oh, fatal Saturday night,
When William Crouch in Marylebone,
  Did slay his innocent wife.

The cause of this dread sad affair.
  As far as we can hear,
This man and wife did disagree,
  Which caused much grief and care,
She vowed the would not live with him,
  Which filled his breast with strife,
And caused him in frenzy for
  To take away her life.

She from her labour was returned,
  And sitting down to rest,
In a neighbour's house as it appears,
  With her infant at her breast,
When her phrenzied husband in a rage,
  To her did go straightway,

With a deadly weapon in his hand
  His innocent wife to slay.

He suddenly her throat did cut,
  And she fell to the floor,
From his lawful wife he took her life,
  Alas ! she was no more,
And when he with the deadly knife,
  Her innocent blood did spill,
He left her weltering in her gore,
  And strove himself to kill.

The neighbourhood was soon alarmed,
  And thousands flocked to see,
The awful spot where William Crouch
  Has caused this tragedy ;
He was quickly apprehended,
  For the murder of his wife,
And put in close confinement
  Upon last Saturday night.

What an awful thing is jealousy,
  With either man or wife,
It was through that this cruel deed,
  Occurred last Saturday night,
Oh, never such a deed again,
  As this may we not see,
And for the present I will end,
  This Marylebone tragedy.

BIRT, Printer, 39, Great St. Andrew Street, Seven Dials.

BROADSIDES

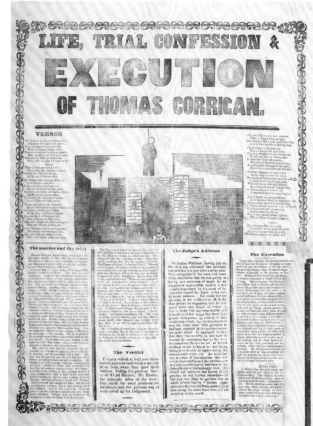

← Broadside for Thomas Corrigan, aged 29, sentenced to be executed for murder, 1856.

Two days before his execution, Corrigan's sentence for the murder of his wife was commuted to transportation on the grounds of insanity. The broadside, printed in advance of the reprieve, erroneously quotes Corrigan's 'last words on the scaffold' as 'When I slew my dear Louisa, / Wandering was my jealous mind.' It also describes his tears upon meeting the executioner, Calcraft, on the scaffold, and the yell he gave as he died. Corrigan received his freedom in 1861 and remained in Australia, becoming a successful journalist.

→ Broadside for John Holland, aged 48, and William King, aged 50, executed at Newgate for sodomy on 25 November 1822.

At the gallows, Holland was observed to 'have a very effeminate voice', 'his screams of anguish being most appalling'. He left a wife and two children. As the 'drop' fell, the crowd shouted, 'Where's the Bishop?' alluding to the Bishop of Clogher who had absconded earlier in 1822 while on bail, having been caught with a young soldier in the Haymarket. Holland and King, as a bricklayer and a labourer, had, presumably, little means or opportunity to abscond. Although officially punishable by death until 1861, execution for sodomy was not enforced after 1835.

TRIAL & EXECUTION,
Of George Coney, Aged 22,

CARPUE, PRINTER.

117, Saffron Hill, Hatton Garden.

WHO SUFFRED THIS MORNING AT NEWGATE.

← Broadside for George Coney, aged 22, executed at Newgate for burglary and robbery, 23 April 1833.

Coney was executed for a burglary in Holborn. The broadside notes that his 15-year-old accomplice was reprieved from execution, most likely owing to his young age. Also printed on the broadside is a letter written on the eve of his execution and a poem, claimed to have been written by Coney, warning 'the young men of London town' against falling into a life of crime.

TRIAL and EXECUTION of
ELIZA ROSS, for the
MURDER of Elizabeth Walsh,
On Friday and Monday January 6th. an 19th. 1832.

QUICK, Printer, 42. Bowing Green Lane, Clerkenwell, London.

EXECUTION

The Sorrowful Lamentation and last farewell to the World of Eliza Ross.

→ Broadside for Eliza Ross, aged 33, executed at Newgate for murder, 9 January 1832.

Ross was executed for the murder of 84-year-old Caroline Walsh, named incorrectly on the broadside as Elizabeth. She and her partner, were accused of 'burking' Walsh, by murdering her and selling her body to surgeons for dissection but only Ross was convicted. The broadside includes the trial evidence of Ross's 12-year-old son, who witnessed the murder.

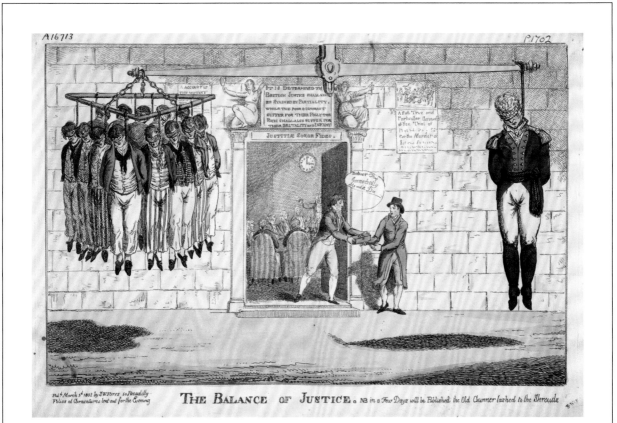

Cartoons and printed images of the executions were also popular souvenirs, particularly for the more infamous crimes. One example is the satirical print produced when military officer Joseph Wall was executed at Newgate on 29 January 1802 for the murder of a soldier who was flogged to death without a trial under his orders. Earlier that month, thirteen mutineer sailors had been hanged at Portsmouth and the print depicts a satirical comparison of the two executions. Wall's brutality made him very unpopular and the government feared the public reaction if he was given a pardon. A huge crowd gave three cheers as the hangman put the noose around Wall's neck.

Published accounts of executions

From the late 17th century, more 'serious' publications began to be produced, such as the Account of the Ordinary of Newgate. The Ordinary regularly spoke to the condemned in their last days. These conversations were summarised and printed for sale, with profits going directly to the Ordinary. The Account was regarded as a more reliable and factual source than the cheaply produced

↑ Satirical print depicting the execution of Joseph Wall and navy mutineers, 1802.

The publisher Samuel William Fores specialised in satirical prints and added the note 'Folios of Caracatures [sic] lent out for the Evening', indicating the popularity of such satirical prints and cartoons at the time.

gallows literature of the street but the words of the condemned could be censored. They were printed regularly for about a hundred years until the late 18th century. The Annals of Newgate, produced in four volumes in 1776, described the crimes and executions of Newgate's most notorious felons. Hugely popular, it was published in many editions and sold throughout the country. Alongside the Bible, the Annals became a standard book in many households. The Newgate Calendar, also published in the 1770s, described individual cases and criminal biographies. Finally, all the cases heard at the Old Bailey were regularly published each time the sessions met as the Proceedings of the Old Bailey. These appeared from 1674 until 1913. They were initially aimed at the general public, but latterly, as newspapers took on much of the reporting of trials, they were read by a much smaller audience of those involved in the legal process.

Refreshments

The sale of food and drink was another important aspect of the execution-day economy. The often-huge crowds spent hours, if not most of a day at the execution site and so were a receptive market for those selling pies, hot potatoes and other refreshments. In the 1850s, there were about 50 piemen in London selling beef, mutton, eel and fruit pies, depending on the season. A regular sight at the Newgate gallows, they set up their charcoal-fired tin cans on stands among the crowds.

↑ *The Coster Boy and Girl Tossing the Pieman, 1864.* The title of this print refers to the habit of tossing a coin with the pieman. If the customer won, they got a free pie. If they lost, they got nothing and the pieman kept the money. The pieman in a top hat stands by his pie can. The can had separate drawers for hot and cold pies and was heated by a charcoal fire.

EXECUTIONERS

Little is known about any of London's medieval executioners. It is only in the late 16th century that they began to be mentioned and then only in terms of their unpopularity. The job of London's common hangman was not one many people wanted to do, and it came with a degree of social ostracisation. Richard Brandon, the probable executioner of King Charles I, inherited the role from his father, Gregory. Inheriting the job, seems to have been the exception rather than the rule, however, and more commonly people came to it having acted as assistant executioner. Many became figures of horror whose names were used to scare children. Most had a reputation for brutality or incompetence and several were criminals themselves. After the late 18th century, the executioner only had to undertake hangings, but until 1747 he had to perform beheadings and, until 1789, burnings.

Executioners often became the focus of the public's hatred, and some lived in fear for their lives. When King Charles I was executed in 1649, the identity of his masked executioner was kept secret. Richard Brandon was the official hangman at the time, and therefore it was assumed that he had carried out the execution. Brandon died a few months later, in June 1649, leaving an alleged deathbed 'confession', claiming he was wracked with guilt. The confession was later published in a pamphlet, which

← The Confession of Richard Brandon, *published 1649.*

also described his funeral, at which the crowd angrily demanded that he should be buried in a dunghill. Brandon was buried at St Mary Whitechapel, to the east of the City of London. The church register recorded the burial of 'Richard Brandon, a man out of Rosemary-lane', to which a later hand added 'supposed to have cut off the head of Charles I'.

One of the most infamous executioners of the 17th century was John 'Jack' Ketch. Although he spent 23 years in the role, his notoriety came from two particularly gruesome executions. In 1683, he took four blows to decapitate Lord William Russell and, in 1685, he took five or more blows to execute the Duke of Monmouth. The following year, Ketch was sent to Bridewell Prison for 'affronting' a sheriff, but was reinstated as executioner after four months when his replacement, Paskah Rose, was himself hanged for murder. The story of Ketch spread and 'Jack Ketch' became a nickname for executioners, as well as the name given to the hangman puppet in Punch and Judy shows.

JACK KETCH ARRESTED
and taken into Custody, when attending a Malefactor to the place of Execution.

The sale of execution relics

Although the common hangman or executioner was paid a fee for each execution, many supplemented their income by selling the clothes of the condemned and other gallows relics, such as pieces of the rope used to hang them. It is said that Brandon was paid £30 (in excess of £75,000 today), for the execution of King Charles I in 1649, but was also allowed to keep a handkerchief and an orange studded with cloves that had belonged to the King. He sold the latter afterwards for ten shillings (over £1,000 today). When Joseph Wall was executed in 1802 for ordering the fatal flogging of a soldier, the notoriety of the case meant that the executioner could sell the rope at a shilling (around £60 today) an inch. Interestingly, a second rope was also sold by a woman said to be the executioner's wife and a third rope was sold in Newgate Street by a merchant at sixpence (around £30 today) an inch. In around 1850, a biography of the hangman William Calcraft alleged

↑ *Jack Ketch being arrested on the way to an execution, 18th century.* This print shows the arrest of the hangman John Price, who was known by the nickname 'Jack Ketch', after the notorious 17th century hangman of that name. Price stands on the back of the cart with his arms raised.
PRINT, 18TH CENTURY.

that a hanging rope could be sold for between five shillings and a pound (the equivalent of between £200 and £900 today) per inch depending on the notoriety of the criminal. By this time, the rope was supplied by the executioner and so was always his to retain after the execution. Pieces of the rope were viewed not just as relics or souvenirs but also as folk cures for illnesses such as epilepsy. The sale of rope for whatever purpose ended in the 1880s when official 'government rope' was supplied for executions.

Making ends meet

As executions took place on about eight days each year, the post of London's executioner was not a full-time occupation. While some held second jobs, others became victims to mounting debts that often landed them in gaol or resorted to robbery, theft or burglary. Two hangmen, John Price and William Marvel, were arrested during their journeys to the gallows. Price was arrested for debt on his way to execute someone and was himself hanged in 1718 for violently attacking Elizabeth White, who died of her injuries. In 1717, Marvel was arrested for debt while he was in Holborn, on his way to Tyburn. In 1719, he was convicted of the theft of ten silk handkerchiefs and was transported to America.

William Calcraft, who was hangman for London and Middlesex from 1829 until 1874, was the longest-serving hangman. He was responsible for the last public execution in London in 1868. He originally trained as a shoemaker or cobbler and during his 45 years of service, he performed an estimated 450 executions. Unlike earlier incumbents, he worked throughout Britain, in part as a result of the newly developed railway system, which made journeys much easier. During this period, as the number of capital crimes decreased, it often became more economical for regional courts to employ London's executioner. Calcraft received about one guinea a week as his executioner's salary, plus a further guinea (in the region of £600 to £1,000 today) for each hanging from the

↓ The Groans of the Gallows, *c.1847.*
This rather lurid account of Calcraft's life was published when he was in his late forties and had already been a hangman for almost 20 years. It included some less than complementary details, such as the allegation that he 'appropriates whatever property might be on the persons of those he executes, including the clothes they die in'.

SECOND EDITION

THE

GROANS OF THE GALLOWS,

OR THE PAST AND PRESENT

LIFE OF

WM. CALCRAFT,

THE LIVING

HANGMAN OF NEWGATE.

ENTERED AT STATIONERS' HALL.

City and Middlesex authorities, plus £5 (between £3,500 and £4,500 today) quarterly from the Surrey authorities. In addition, he could charge in the region of £10 (between about £7,000 and £9,000 today) for executions outside London. He then further topped up his salary by selling pieces of the execution rope or the clothes of the executed, sometimes to waxworks for display.

Calcraft was notorious for his preference for the short-drop method of hanging which usually led to the condemned slowly strangling to death. During his period in office, research in Ireland led to the development of the long-drop method, but this was only adopted in England after Calcraft retired in 1874, when he was aged about 74. A number of accounts of his life were published while he was still alive. These included many details that added to his dubious reputation.

CHAPTER 5

Burial / Dissection / Death masks / Gibbeting /
The display of body parts / Mourning and remembering / Life after death

THE EXECUTED BODY

While the majority of those executed were buried, the public nature of executions meant that punishment for serious crimes continued after death. The heads and body parts of traitors were displayed in public places. The corpses of murderers, highway robbers and pirates were hung in gibbet cages alongside main roads, on commons and by the River Thames. Surgeons dissected the bodies of murderers in front of paying audiences and displayed their skeletons. Casts of the heads of notorious murderers were exhibited and studied in an attempt to learn about their characters.

The tradition that the hanged body could have curative properties had been strongly held since medieval times. In particular, stroking the hand of a hanged man was regarded as a popular cure for a range of skin and other ailments. This appears to have become more commonplace after the mid 18th century and continued for about 100 years. The *Morning Post* of 20 September 1825 reported the following occurrence after the execution of Patrick Welch in front of Newgate, for the murder of his wife:

> *...after untying the wrists of the deceased, an old woman, nearly 70 years of age, attended by a youth, stepped on the scaffold: the executioner placed his arm round her neck, and proceeded to rub it with the hand of the malefactor; he continued to do this until the poor old lady had nearly fainted away, when he desisted, but, after the lapse of a short time, renewed his exertions with the other hand. When he had finished, the woman put on her bonnet and shawl, and coolly walked off the scaffold.*

The aim of this scene had been to cure a boil or swelling that the woman had on one side of her neck. As can be seen from this description, the touching could not happen without the help of the executioner, and it was yet another service for which he charged. This case from 1825, appears to be the final time it happened in London, although the tradition continued for some time elsewhere in the country.

BURIAL

Most executed people were buried in the churchyard of their parish church. Those without friends or family to claim their bodies were buried in pits near the gallows. Human skeletal remains have been uncovered during building work around the site of Tyburn for over 200 years. By the later 18th century, it was common for criminals to be buried in quicklime within Newgate Prison itself. The burial site was a passageway known as Birdcage Walk or Dead Man's Walk. The bodies were interred beneath the flagstones of the passageway and the location marked with the initial of the individual's surname. In 1904, when the prison was demolished, over 90 skeletons were reburied in the City of London cemetery.

For the poor, the cost of a funeral was not inconsiderate, and so it could sometimes be difficult to find someone to take the body.

↓ *Keys to Newgate Prison 'burying ground', late 18th century.*
The executed could be buried in Newgate alongside those who died in prison. These keys provided access to the burial site.

In May 1762, the *Bath Chronicle and Weekly Gazette* reported that the body of a man who was hanged for mutiny at Execution Dock was taken to relations in both Whitechapel and Spitalfields, but they refused to bury him. In the end, friends of his brought the body to an empty house where it was displayed to the public at 2 pence (about £15 today) per person until enough money had been raised for the burial. At the other end of the scale, funerals for people who had attracted great public sympathy could become major events, attended by thousands.

DISSECTION

The link between dissection and execution in Britain has its origins in the mid 16th century. In 1540, during the reign of

King Henry VIII, the founding charter of
the Company of Barber-Surgeons specified
the supply of four executed bodies each year
to the Company for anatomical dissection.
From 1565, both the Company and the
College of Physicians were allowed a limited
number of corpses of hanged individuals for
dissection. Fights would sometimes break
out at executions as the friends and family of
the deceased would try to stop the surgeons
claiming the body. The thought of being
dissected filled most people with horror, as it
meant they would not receive a proper burial.
There were also other concerns, as illustrated
by the case of William Duell. In 1740, Duell,
who was about 17 years old, was sentenced
to death for the rape and robbery of Sarah
Griffin. At Tyburn, he was hanged for the
customary hour, before his body was cut down
and removed to Surgeons' Hall for dissection.
He was heard to groan, and the surgeons
revived him and returned him to Newgate.
His sentence was eventually commuted to
transportation.

Over time, the demand for bodies to
be medically dissected far outweighed
the supply. In the 18th century, a more punitive approach to
execution developed. The Murder Act 1752 sought in part to
address these two issues. It mandated that the bodies of executed
murderers should not be buried but should be either publicly
dissected or 'hung in chains' (gibbeted). This, the Act stated,
would add 'some further terror and peculiar mark of infamy'
to capital punishment, 'better preventing the horrid crime of
murder'. It thus provided anatomists with a supply of cadavers
to dissect and expose to members of the public who paid a fee to
view the procedure. Under the Act, those murderers executed
in London and Middlesex who were sent for dissection would
be taken to the new Surgeons' Hall, which had opened that same
year near the Old Bailey. The practice stopped in 1832 with the
introduction of the Anatomy Act.

The 1752 Act did not differentiate by class, meaning that
members of the aristocracy could meet the same fate as paupers.

↑ *The body of Earl Ferrers*
in his coffin before his
dissection at Surgeons'
Hall, 1760.
PRINT, 1795.

'He had such a
dread of falling
into the hands of
the surgeons, that
he sent letters
to several of his
acquaintance,
begging they would
rescue his body...'
New and Complete
Newgate Calendar, 1795

MURDER ON A TRAIN

Franz Müller, aged 24, executed on 14 November 1864

Franz Müller, a German tailor, was the first person to commit a murder on a British railway. He robbed and beat Thomas Briggs and threw him out of a North London train, between Bow and Hackney Wick. Briggs died shortly afterwards from his injuries. Müller fled to America and was arrested in New York after a Scotland Yard inspector, Richard Tanner, followed him across the Atlantic. Tanner's ship was much faster than the one that Müller was on, allowing him to reach New York ahead of Müller and to arrest him on arrival. Müller was then brought back for trial at the Old Bailey. The murder, investigation, chase across the Atlantic and Müller's eventual trial and execution created a sensation and huge popular interest. After his execution, Müller was buried under the flagstones of Birdcage Walk in Newgate Prison. The *British Standard* reported:

Towards the middle of the day the rough deal box which held it [Müller's body], was filled with shavings and quick lime, and the warders carried it to the hole where it had to be thrust under the flagstones of a narrow, bleak, gaol pathway... there, where none pass the little hidden grave save those who, like himself, must go over it to their own great doom, the body of Müller rests. In a few days... will be commemorated by a rough 'M.' cut in the gaol stone near his head.

↑ *Broadside about the trial and execution of Franz Müller, for the murder of Mr Thomas Briggs, 1864.*

This broadside describes the huge crowd that came to watch Müller's execution on 14 November 1864.

BURIALS AT TYBURN

Archaeological evidence from Marble Arch

Between 1961 and 1962, new pedestrian subways were built at Marble Arch. Construction workers, monitored by archaeologists, found large quantities of human bones. These were probably the remains of executed people who had been buried at the site of the Tyburn gallows, not having anyone to claim their bodies. There are several accounts of bodies dumped in pits at Tyburn, including those of the Catholic martyrs John Roberts and Thomas Somers, who were buried with sixteen other 'condemned persons' in 1610. One of the skeletons still had a pair of iron shackles around their ankles.

↑ *Iron shackles found attached to the leg bones of an individual buried at Tyburn.*
Found during the 1961 archaeological investigations at Tyburn, these iron shackles are a macabre reminder of the reality of conditions for prisoners.

↓ *Archaeological drawing of the 1961 excavations at Marble Arch.*
The outline of the hexagonal toll house and the site of the Triple Tree are marked, along with the locations of the human remains that were uncovered.

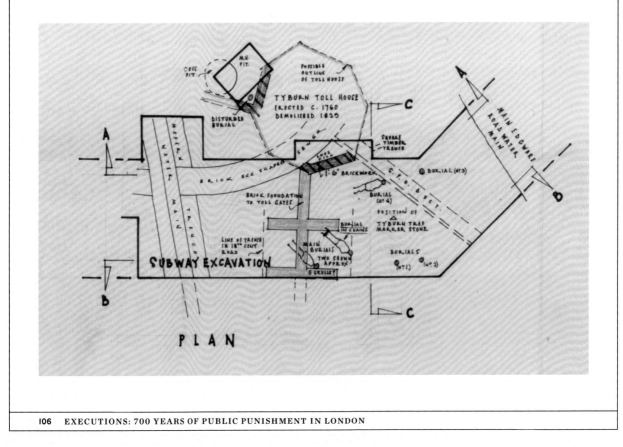

THE REWARD OF CRUELTY.

Behold the Villain's dire disgrace!
Not Death itself can end.
He finds no peaceful Burial-Place,
His breathless Corse, no friend.

Torn from the Root, that wicked Tongue,
Which daily swore and curst!
Those Eyeballs from their Sockets wrung,
That glow'd with lawless Lust!

His Heart expos'd to prying Eyes,
To Pity has no Claim:
But, dreadful! from his Bones shall rise,
His Monument of Shame.

This was quite fascinating for many members of the public. After Earl Ferrers was hanged in 1760, his body was taken to Surgeons' Hall in a satin-lined coffin where it was put on public show. A 'great number of spectators' came to watch the surgeons 'anatomise' him; it was the first time an aristocrat had been dissected after execution. His body was cut open and his bowels were removed but it was not fully dissected, on account of his noble status. He was buried secretly at St Pancras Church. Such 'formal' dissections – usually meaning that the corpse was cut open but not fully eviscerated – were often used on the bodies of the more well-to-do.

In certain cases, the skeletons were retained and put on display in Surgeons' Hall. In 1824, a newspaper described 'several niches at this anatomical theatre for the skeletons of remarkable

DRAWING THE DEAD

Written and sketched 'Records of the heads of murderers' were kept by the Royal College of Surgeons between 1807 and 1832. These drawings were made by William Clift (1775–1849) and his son, William Home Clift (1803–33). Clift senior also performed the dissections of murderers at the Royal College of Surgeons where he worked as an illustrator and conservator. He was very skilled at dissecting, and his notes on dissections contain many anatomical observations, but his drawings of the heads of murderers rarely have any obvious scientific purpose, serving rather as post-mortem portraits. Clift used red crayon in some of his sketches to highlight the deep red welts that the noose imprinted around the necks of the executed. Most of his sketches are inscribed with the subject's name and the date of their execution. Many also contain details of the crime for which they were condemned. This information was of no scientific significance, but instead bears witness to an interest in criminal lives that seems to have been shared by the public and the anatomists alike, raising the question of just what the purpose of these drawings really was: artistic, administrative, commemorative or sheer curiosity?

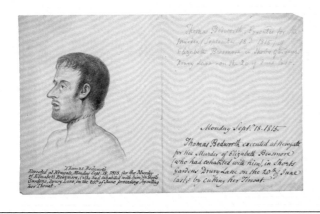

← *Thomas Bedworth, executed at Newgate, for the murder of Elizabeth Beesmore, 18 September 1815.*

Bedworth had been living with Elizabeth Beesmore but they had separated. Having been drinking, he went to her lodgings in Shorts Gardens, off Drury Lane, and cut her throat. He then absconded, walking to Coventry, where he handed himself in, and was returned to London to stand trial.

DRAWING BY WILLIAM CLIFT, 18 SEPTEMBER 1815.

← *David Evans, executed at Newgate for the murder of his wife, Elizabeth, 23 February 1818.*

Clift's notes on this sketch of David Evans demonstrate a judgemental attitude towards the behaviour of the condemned man in his final hours: 'This cowardly ruffian wished to hurry the time of Execution, being afraid of being left alone with his Wife's Ghost.'

DRAWING BY WILLIAM CLIFT, 23 FEBRUARY 1818.

← *Esther Hibner, executed at Newgate for the murder of her apprentice, Frances Colpit, 13 April 1830.*

Esther Hibner's case attracted considerable public attention because of the great cruelty of her crime: mistreating and starving to death her 12-year-old apprentice. Her notoriety is hinted at in the notes accompanying this portrait. After an initial examination, her body was sent to Guy's Hospital where Dr Bright examined the brain. Such gifts to selected surgeons and students became an important way for the Royal College of Surgeons to cultivate professional relationships with London's scientific community.

DRAWING BY WILLIAM HOME CLIFT, 13 APRIL 1830.

← *William Sawyer, executed at Newgate for the murder of Harriet Gaskett, 15 May 1815.*

Sawyer, an officer posted to Lisbon, had shot his lover and then attempted to take his own life, by shooting himself and later trying to cut his throat. Unlike the other portraits displayed here, Sawyer's head faces right, presumably to show the bullet wound where he had attempted to kill himself.

DRAWING BY WILLIAM CLIFT, 15 MAY 1815.

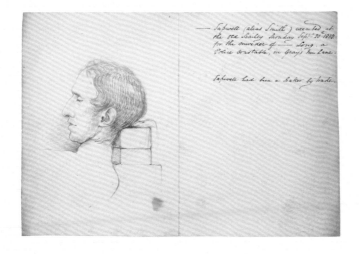

← *John Smith, alias William Sapwell, executed at Newgate for the murder of a policeman, John Long, 20 September 1830.*

This self-assured and almost tender drawing makes use of Smith's profile to capture his individuality, and gives the impression of a deathbed portrait rather than of a biological illustration. PC Long was the second member of the newly formed Metropolitan Police force to be murdered in the line of duty when he died in August 1830.

DRAWING BY WILLIAM HOME CLIFT, 20 SEPTEMBER 1830.

culprits of this description [i.e. murderers]', including Thomas Wilford, who had one arm, and had been executed for the murder of his wife in 1752, and Elizabeth Brownrigg, executed in 1767 for the murder of her female apprentice.

DEATH MASKS

Death masks of executed murderers were made for the purpose of research. Although known as masks, these were more often full casts of the head. Students of phrenology compared the shape and size of the skulls to determine characteristics of the criminal mind. Phrenology – now held to be pseudoscience – was developed by Franz Joseph Gall and Johann Gaspar Spurzheim in the late 18th and early 19th centuries. Gall believed that different areas of the brain corresponded with different personality traits, and that the size of these areas not only indicated their strength but affected

'A shelf, on which were a few boxes for papers, and casts of the heads and faces of the two notorious murderers, Bishop and Williams; the former, in particular, exhibiting a style of head and set of features, which might have afforded sufficient moral grounds for his instant execution at any time, even had there been no other evidence against him.'
Charles Dickens, author, 1836

the shape of the head. He examined a number of murderers' skulls and concluded that the area above their ears was larger than normal, perhaps indicating a propensity to kill. This was later called the 'organ of destructiveness' by Spurzheim. Gall's theories grew in popularity during the early 19th century, but by the 1840s they were beginning to be discredited. Advances in neuroscience showed that while the brain was spatially organised, it was not in the way the phrenologists believed, and not with any correlation to the size and shape of the skull.

Not all of the casts were kept in scientific collections and some were retained more as macabre souvenirs. A number of casts depicting notorious criminals were on display in Newgate Prison, where they formed a part of tours for important visitors or those who were able to gain a permit. At the time of Dickens's visit in 1836, there appear to have only been two casts in a room with a desk and a visitors' book at the start of the tour. By 1873, when the illustration for *The Illustrated London News* was made, there were two shelves crowded with heads in a room to the left of the gatekeeper's lodge, but by the 1890s they appear to have been kept in a cupboard. At the 1903 auction of the contents of Newgate, it was reported: 'Of the weird plaster casts, nine in number, the less said the better. They made one or two ladies sick, and their exposure only resulted in five guineas.'

Once the condemned had been hanged, their body was brought back into Newgate, the head was shorn and 'smeared with oil

↓ *Phrenology head, c.1840.*

GUILTY OF INFANTICIDE

Catherine Welch, aged 24, executed on 14 April 1828

Catherine Welch (or Welsh) was convicted of murder after the body of a baby who was about six weeks old was found in a ditch. A doctor concluded that she had recently given birth by examining her breasts, pressing them and finding that they were still expressing breast milk. Welch confirmed this but denied murder, claiming her child had died of natural causes two months earlier and been buried. The jury found her guilty on circumstantial evidence, but were so concerned that the evidence used to convict her was unsound that they recommended a reprieve. One of the jurors, Thomas Flather, felt 'much distressed', writing to the Home Secretary, Sir Robert Peel on 13 April 1828: 'I certainly censure myself in the strongest manner for submitting to a verdict of guilty.' Despite the jury's sympathy, relatively few people signed Catherine's petition. As a new arrival to the capital from Ireland, she was 'without friends' to help her.

Welch confessed to the murder a few days before her execution to the Catholic priest sent to pray with her, explaining that she was unable to support her child after her husband abandoned her. She had married him when already pregnant by another man. When the baby arrived, he realised it wasn't his. She claimed that he told her he would only return to her if she got rid of the baby. Welch's case is a reminder of the speed at which punishments were meted out: she was tried at the Old Bailey on the 10 April 1828, and executed on 14 April 1828.

After execution, her body was sent for dissection and was drawn by William Home Clift. Once a 'proper examination' had been made at the Royal College of Surgeons, it was sent to Charles Bell's private anatomy school in Windmill Street, after which her breasts were removed for preservation in the College Museum. The body of a woman who had recently given birth was particularly prized as it could be used to demonstrate female anatomy at a time when decorum dictated that doctors should examine female patients by touch alone without seeing their genitalia.

← *Catherine Welch.*
William Home Clift undertook this drawing of Welch's body at the Royal College of Surgeons. As her body was going to a private anatomy school for full dissection, the College's examination would have been fairly perfunctory. The private anatomists were supposed to send full medical reports of their dissections to the College, but in Welch's case they did not, a cause of some annoyance to the College.
DRAWN BY WILLIAM HOME CLIFT, 14 APRIL 1828.

and a plaster cast taken of it.' The casts were made from plaster of Paris and were the work of a number of skilled artists and craftsmen. The cast of Luigi Buranelli's head was made by the Italian-born moulder and figure-maker Bartholomew Casci at his workshop in Drury Lane. Robert Blakesley's head was crafted by James Deville (1777–1846), an expert plaster cast-maker who studied phrenology. He opened his first plaster works in Soho in 1803, later moving to Leicester Square and then the Strand as his success grew. A co-founder of the London Phrenological Society, Deville also made casts of living subjects including 48 convicts awaiting transportation to the penal colonies. Both Gall and Spurzheim thought highly of Deville's work. At his death in 1846, he had over 5,000 head casts and skulls stored at his premises in the Strand.

GIBBETING

'Hanging in chains' – or gibbeting – was an extra punishment used for crimes such as highway robbery, piracy, smuggling, robbing the mail and murder. The criminal's dead body would be put in an iron cage and hung from a gibbet, a vertical pole with a horizontal arm from which the cage would be suspended, often for many years. Occasionally gibbets were erected near the sites of the crime in London, but it was more common to see gibbets on the heaths and along the highways on the outskirts of the

'...from whatever quarter the wind blew, it brought with it a cadaverous and pestilential odour. The nation is becoming more civilised; they now take the bodies down after reasonable exposure...'

Robert Southey, poet, 1802

↓ *Gibbet at Blackwall Reach, 1782.*

The gibbet can be seen on the far shore, to the right of the ship.

ENGRAVING PUBLISHED IN THE LONDON MAGAZINE, MARCH 1782.

Dodd delin?.   Malpas sculp?.

View of HOUNSLOW HEATH, *with the* GIBETS
and Men hanging in Chains

← *Gibbet cage, 18th century.*
This reusable gibbet was adjustable for different-sized bodies. The Admiralty placed cages such as this next to the Thames, to display the bodies of people who had committed crimes at sea.

← *Warning sign for a gibbet, 1701–2.*
This painted notice threatens 'Death or transportation the penalty for any interference with this gibbet'. It was put up under the orders of William Withers, Sheriff of London.

capital or along the river. From 1752, all murderers were ordered to be dissected or gibbeted after execution to deter crime and demonstrate justice and the power of the state. Between 1726 and 1830, at least 38 out of the 87 men convicted of capital crimes by the Admiralty Court were gibbeted after their execution. Most were placed at various points along the River Thames east of London, especially at bends in the river like Blackwall Reach, where they would be more visible to boats entering the city. In 1824, William Dykes complained to the Home Secretary, Sir Robert Peel, of the 'revolting spectacle exhibited on the banks of the Thames'. More people were gibbeted in London than anywhere else. The poet Robert Southey made the exaggerated claim that in the 1770s there had been 'a hundred such [corpses] exposed upon the heath'. The practice was abolished in 1834.

People were both disgusted and fascinated by the sight. Huge crowds visited new gibbets, buying sausages and gingerbread from food sellers, and gin from temporary drinking booths. William Smith's gibbet on Finchley Common was visited by 40,000 people on the Sunday after his execution in 1782.

While some gibbet cages were reusable, most were made for individual criminals. The blacksmith would measure them before their execution, an experience that could make the most hardened criminal break down in fear. Their dead, rotting body would hang in the cage for years. Gibbet cages were hung from poles that were 30 feet (over 9 metres) high to prevent people

← *Gibbets on Hounslow Heath, c.1790.*
ENGRAVED BY MALPAS AFTER DANIEL DODD, C.1790.

← *Heads of traitors on London Bridge, 1616.*
A close inspection of this bird's-eye view of London Bridge from Southwark reveals the heads of traitors mounted on spikes on the gate leading onto the bridge from the south.
ENGRAVING BY JOHN VISSCHER, REPRINTED IN 1840–60.

'*At the top of one tower almost in the centre of the [London] bridge, were stuck on tall stakes more than thirty skulls of noble men who had been executed and beheaded for treason and for other reasons.*'

Thomas Platter the Younger, physician and diarist, 1599

Views of the CITY GATES as they appeared before they were pulled down, together with the OLD GATE at WHITEHALL & TEMPLEBAR.

climbing or tampering with them. Warning signs were posted on them aimed at stopping people from stealing the bodies either for burial or to sell for dissection, or taking pieces as ghoulish mementoes.

THE DISPLAY OF BODY PARTS

After execution, it was not uncommon for parts of the body of the executed person to be displayed in public. Gateways and bridges were favoured locations, where these gruesome memorials would be seen by those entering and exiting the City of London. Until the 18th century, London Bridge was the only bridge across the River Thames in London and one of the main routes into the City. The decapitated heads of traitors were displayed there as a warning against rebellion. Sir William Wallace, the Scottish freedom fighter, is the first recorded person to be punished this way – his head was displayed in 1305. The Catholic William Staley, victim of the Popish Plot in 1678, was the last. The only woman's head displayed on the bridge was that of Elizabeth Barton, in 1534. Known as the Maid of Kent, she had preached against Henry VIII's annulment of his marriage to his first wife, Catherine

↑ Views of the City Gates, the old gate at Whitehall and Temple Bar, 18th century.

Spikes bearing heads can be seen on Temple Bar, a gate across Fleet Street. These heads are the remains of the Jacobite rebels executed in 1746.

ETCHING BY J.G. WOODING, PUBLISHED BY ALEXANDER HOGG, 1784.

of Aragon and was found guilty of treason and executed at Tyburn.

Heads were also placed on the gates leading into the City of London. Samuel Pepys noted in his diary on 20 October 1660: 'I saw the limbs of some of our new traitors set upon Aldersgate, which was a sad sight to see.' These were men executed by King Charles II in revenge for their part in the death of his father, King Charles I. Another location for displaying decapitated heads was Temple Bar gate, on Fleet Street, which marked the politically significant entrance to the City from Westminster. Francis Towneley and George Fletcher were two of the nine officers of the Jacobite Manchester Regiment to be executed as traitors on Kennington Common on 30 July 1746. After they had been hanged and decapitated, their heads became the last to be displayed on pikes on Temple Bar. Towneley's head was later returned to his family, in whose possession it remained until it was finally buried in the 1940s.

MOURNING AND REMEMBERING

Some of those executed were seen as victims of miscarriages of justice or of a harsh and arbitrary legal system that punished them too severely. In high-profile cases, mourning could become a major public event. The funeral of Eliza Fenning was attended by around 10,000 people in 1815. Some mourners became public figures, made famous by their displays of grief. Executed rebels could become martyrs, their memories and the causes they died for kept alive through relics and mementoes venerated by their families and allies.

Some of these relics were items that had belonged to the condemned. Before Sir John Fenwick was beheaded for treason on Tower Hill, he gave his snuffbox to his solicitor, Christopher

Observe the Banner which would all enslave
Which ruined Traytors did so proudly wave
The Devil seems the project to despise
A Fiend confused from off the trophy flies.

While trembling Rebels at the Fabrick gaze
And dread their fate with horror and amaze
Let Britons Sons the Emblematick view
And plainly see what is Rebellions due.

↑ *Temple Bar with the heads of Francis Towneley and George Fletcher, 1746.*

The heads of Towneley and Fletcher can be seen on spikes on the gate, while a devil looms over them, holding a banner reading 'A Crown or A Grave'. The masks of the two dead men appear to the left and right of the scene.

LITHOGRAPH BY DAY & SON AFTER AN ETCHING OF 1746, C.1830–5.

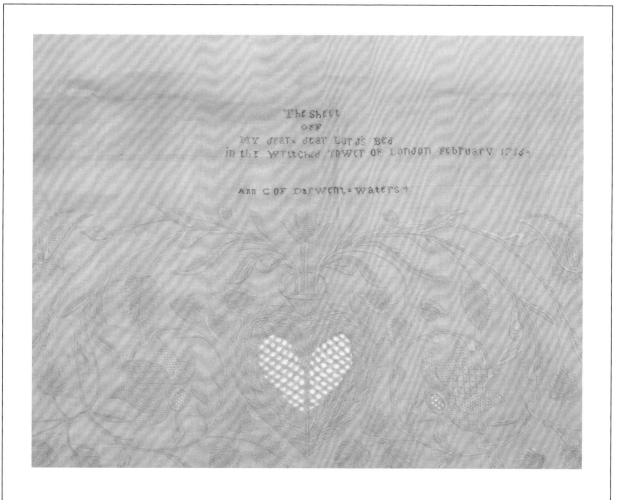

'The sheet
off
my dear, dear Lord's bed
in the wretched Tower of London February 1716.

Ann C of Darwent-Waters +

Dighton. Fenwick had conspired to put King James II back
on the throne in place of King William III. His efforts to save
himself by confessing details of the plot failed and he was
executed on 28 January 1697. Other mementoes were intensely
private and personal. In 1716, when the 26-year-old Jacobite
rebel James Radclyffe, the Earl of Derwentwater, was executed
as a traitor, his widow, Anna Maria, kept a bed sheet that he had
used while a prisoner in the Tower of London. She embroidered
the sheet as a way of dealing with her grief and stitched the
lettering using human hair. The wording on the sheet reads:
'The sheet off my dear, dear Lord's bed in the wretched Tower
of London, February 1716, Ann C of Derwent-Waters'. The hair
used may have been her own or her husband's, or possibly from
both of them, as analysis indicates both a fairer and darker hair
being used (portraits indicate that her hair was much darker
than his). Until January 1716, Anna Maria was allowed to share
her husband's quarters in the Tower and she may have cut locks

↑ *The bed sheet (detail)*
of James Radclyffe,
Earl of Derwentwater,
embroidered by his widow,
Anna Maria, 1716.

The sheet is made from
two widths of closely
woven linen joined by a
seam. The top and bottom
edges are hemmed and
decorated with bands
of embroidery in linen
thread (flowers, leaves and
geometric patterns), and
human hair (lettering).

POISONER OR INNOCENT VICTIM?

Eliza Fenning, executed on 26 July 1815

Eliza Fenning, a domestic cook in her early 20s, worked for the Turner family in Chancery Lane. In March 1815, several members of the household, including Fenning, fell ill after eating dumplings she had made. Traces of arsenic were found in the mixture, and Fenning was arrested for attempting to poison her employers. She maintained her innocence throughout her trial and imprisonment. The evidence against her was questionable and public opinion was in her favour. However, she was found guilty and hanged on 26 July after efforts to petition for mercy failed.

Young, pretty and possibly innocent, Eliza Fenning captured the public's imagination. After she was hanged, many people visited her body at her parents' house, lying 'in her coffin seemingly as in a sweet sleep, with a smile on her countenance'. Around 10,000 people were thought to have attended her funeral, which began with a huge procession to the church, accompanied by police officers to keep the peace.

Many pamphlets, newspaper articles, ballads and books were published about Eliza Fenning's case. One of the books was by John Watkins who was appalled by the apparent miscarriage of justice. He included extra evidence to support Fenning's claim of innocence, a detailed account of her execution and letters written by her during her imprisonment. The book warns that the law should be scrutinised to avoid similar abuses.

I.R. Cruikshank fecit.

ELIZABETH FENNING,
Executed 26. July 1815, on a charge of
POISONING THE FAMILY OF MR TURNER,
taken from the Life in Newgate.

Her Autograph. *Elizabeth Fenning*

Publish'd August 1815. by W. HONE, 55. Fleet St.

↑ *Portrait of Eliza Fenning, 1815.*
ENGRAVING BY ISAAC ROBERT CRUIKSHANK, PUBLISHED BY WILLIAM HONE, 1815.

of his hair then, or later when his body was returned to the family for burial. When she died, she left a lock of the Earl's hair to their daughter.

A more public memento of the Earl were the printed copies of the speech he gave on the scaffold before his beheading. He had supported James Stuart, the Old Pretender, to be king of England instead of King George I. In his speech, he apologised for pleading guilty to treason, saying his only loyalty was to James (whom he called James III in his speech). He also said that he died a Roman Catholic and hoped that his death would help in the campaign to put James on the throne. Following Anna Maria's own early death in 1723, the bed sheet became a symbol and relic of Catholic martyrdom.

The lives of those who grieved for executed loved ones were rarely recorded. But one individual who became well known precisely because of her bereavement was Sarah Whitehead. In 1812, her brother Paul, a clerk at the Bank of England, was executed for forgery. For the next 40 years, Sarah, attired in a black dress and veil, frequently visited the bank to ask if her brother was there. Bank employees humoured her and gave her small sums of money, calling her the Bank Nun.

LIFE AFTER DEATH

While many of the condemned were forgotten by all but those who knew them or were involved in their crime, the lives and stories, or sometimes just the names, of certain individuals lived on after they were executed. For an even smaller number, their names passed into legend, and their stories were told and retold through books and pamphlets long after they had died, fuelling Londoners' obsession with criminality. The more heinous the crime, the more sensational the retelling, particularly if women were the perpetrators. The case of Elizabeth Sawyer in 1621, inspired a play, *The Witch of Edmonton*, which was performed later the same year at the Cockpit Theatre in Drury Lane. Sawyer, from Winchmore Hill, Enfield, was hanged at Tyburn for the murder of her neighbour Agnes Ratcleife by witchcraft. Sawyer was a poor woman with a stooped back and only one eye. She pleaded not guilty but later confessed that

↑ *Sir John Fenwick's snuffbox, 1697.*
The horn snuffbox given by Sir John Fenwick to his solicitor, Christopher Dighton, before his execution.

↓ *The last speech of James Radclyffe, Earl of Derwentwater, beheaded on Tower Hill, 1716.*

[3]

THE
SPEECH
OF
James Earl of Darwentwater.
Who was Beheaded on Tower Hill for High Treason against His Majesty K. George, Febr. 24. 1715-16.

Eing in a few Minutes to appear before the Tribunal of God, where, tho' most unworthy, I hope to find Mercy which I have not found from Men in Power, I have endeavoured to make my Peace with His Divine Majesty, by most humbly begging Pardon for all the Sins of my Life; and I doubt not of a merciful Forgiveness, through the Merits of the Passion and Death of my Saviour Jesus Christ, for which end I earnestly desire the Prayers of all good Christians

After

the Devil had appeared to her as a black dog called Tom. In 1848, the crimes of Harriet Parker, who killed her lover's children, and Annette Meyers, who murdered a soldier in St James's Park, were published together in a cheap pamphlet called *The Execution of Female Murderers*. It included a moral verse claimed to have been written by Meyers warning 'females young to guard against the pangs of love and men's deluding tongue'.

Images of the condemned were cheaply printed and circulated. Others ended up modelled in wax, starring in the many waxworks that toured Britain in the 19th century. A number donated their clothes to Madame Tussauds and other public waxwork exhibitions, so that their figures would be authentic. The Tussauds were known to buy the entire contents of a room where a murder had taken place. After her execution in 1832, a full-length wax model of Eliza Ross was displayed, wearing clothes which, if not the exact ones, were faithful copies of those worn at her execution. Her figure had been sculpted by Mr Samo and was exhibited with other figures by Mr Simmons at rooms in Finsbury Square and later in High Holborn.

↙ *Sarah Whitehead, the 'Bank Nun', c.1850.* LITHOGRAPHY, C.1850–1900.

↓ *The title page of* **The Witch of Edmonton** *by William Rowley, Thomas Dekker and John Ford, 1658.* Central to Elizabeth Sawyer's case and to the play was the devil-dog, Tom. In the play, Sawyer is depicted as a poor, lonely figure worthy of the audience's pity. This was unusual at a time when witch trials were rife and sympathy for women accused of witchcraft was limited.

THE LATE
MISS WHITEHEAD,
THE
BANK NUN.

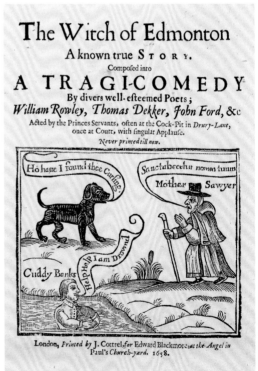

The Witch of Edmonton
A known true STORY.
Composed into
A TRAGI-COMEDY
By divers well-esteemed Poets;
William Rowley, Thomas Dekker, John Ford, &c
Acted by the Princes Servants, often at the Cock-Pit in Drury-Lane,
once at Court, with singular Applause.
Never printed till now.

Ho have I found thee Curse?
Sanctabecetur nomen tuum
Mother Sawyer
Help help I am Drown'd
Cuddy Banks

London, Printed by J. Cottrel, for Edward Blackmore, at the Angel in
Paul's Church-yard. 1658.

FAME ...

John 'Jack' Sheppard, aged 22, executed on 16 November 1724

The thief John 'Jack' Sheppard was one of London's greatest criminal heroes. A series of ingenious escapes from prison made Sheppard a London celebrity and he became a symbol of freedom for London's working classes. An apprentice carpenter, he fell into a life of thieving, led astray by bad company and lewd women. Having escaped from prison four times, he was eventually executed in 1724 at the age of 22. His procession to Tyburn was accompanied by a distraught and sympathetic crowd.

Sheppard was already infamous before the artist Sir James James Thornhill paid one shilling and sixpence to visit him in his cell to draw his portrait. An autobiographical account of his life, produced with Sheppard's agreement, and probably ghostwritten by Daniel Defoe, was produced in time to be sold at his execution.

His effrontery and skill in challenging authority ensured that his fame grew over the following 150 years with numerous plays, chapbooks (small cheaply made books or pamphlets) and prints being produced. He was the inspiration for John Gay's play *The Beggar's Opera*, first performed in 1728. After a lull, his story again became popular in the early 19th century. In 1839, William Ainsworth's novel about Sheppard was published in serial form in *Bentley's Miscellany* with illustrations by George Cruikshank. The author confidently predicted: 'The success of Jack is pretty certain, they are bringing him out at half the theatres in London.' The authorities, however, attempted to ban the plays, fearing their popularity would encourage a crime wave among London's youths.

In the 1850s, Henry Mayhew discovered that chapbooks recounting Sheppard's exploits were hugely popular in poorer lodging houses where they were read aloud to illiterate youths. He interviewed thirteen boys who confessed to thieving in order to pay for a theatre ticket for the play about Jack's life.

← ← *Jack Sheppard, 1724.*
Sheppard, his hands manacled, sits in his prison cell, looking towards the window. This sympathetic portrait by Thornhill was done in Sheppard's cell shortly before his execution. It was widely copied as an engraving.
DRAWING BY SIR JAMES THORNHILL, 1724.

← Jack Sheppard
chapbook, 1820–30.
PUBLISHED, C.1820–30.

... AND INFAMY

Elizabeth Brownrigg, aged 47, executed on 14 September 1767

Midwife Elizabeth Brownrigg, her husband and son carried out a long regime of abuse on three young female apprentices, Mary Jones, Mary Mitchell and 14-year-old Mary Clifford who had been placed with the Brownriggs by the Foundling Hospital. The girls were regularly stripped, badly beaten and locked in a cellar. Jones escaped in 1765 and Mitchell survived. Clifford received the worst of the beatings and died of her injuries. Brownrigg's husband and son were sentenced to six months' imprisonment in Newgate Prison, while Brownrigg herself was sentenced to death. On the morning of her execution on 14 September 1767, her husband and son were allowed to join her in the chapel at Newgate to pray and receive Communion.

London society was horrified by Brownrigg's brutal crime, and thousands gathered to watch her being taken to Tyburn to be hanged. The newspapers reported that people were injured in the crush and had their pockets picked. The crowd shouted 'hellish curses' at her and cried, 'Pull off her hat, that we may see the bitch's face.' After her death, her body was dissected and her skeleton was displayed in a niche at Surgeons' Hall next to Newgate so that 'the heinousness of her cruelty might make the more lasting impression on the minds of the spectators'. Her cruel and abusive treatment of her young female apprentices was thought to be totally out of character for a woman. 'Mother Brownrigg' became a notorious figure of evil for many years.

↗ *Murderer Elizabeth Brownrigg at Newgate Prison, 1767.*
ENGRAVING AFTER NATHANIEL DANCE, 1767.

→ *The skeleton of Elizabeth Brownrigg in Surgeons' Hall, 1795.*
PRINT, 1795.

Jack Sheppard taken from Newgate.

Blueskin attempting to Rescue Jack Sheppard on Holborn Hill.

Jack Sheppard drinking from the St. Giles's Bowl.

Jack Sheppard's Farewell to M.r Wood.

Blueskin cutting down Jack Sheppard.

The body of Jack Sheppard carried off by the Mob.

← *Jack Sheppard's journey to Tyburn and execution.*
Part of a collection of 27 etchings by George Cruikshank from W. H. Ainsworth's *Jack Sheppard*, published in 1839, these images show Sheppard on his journey to Tyburn and then his execution on the Triple Tree. Huge crowds can be seen surrounding the scaffold and seated in the stands.
ETCHINGS BY GEORGE CRUIKSHANK, 1839.

CHAPTER 6

*Transportation / Prison reform /
The establishment of the Metropolitan Police Force /
Criticism of public execution / The last public execution in London*

ENDING THE SPECTACLE

By the 1860s, public execution was increasingly at odds with ambitions to modernise London. As the city's landscape changed, so did society. Public violence and pain became unacceptable to Victorian sensitivities. Social reformers questioned the morality of the execution crowd and the effectiveness of public execution as a deterrent. The decline in capital offences and the founding of the Metropolitan Police brought new approaches towards crime and punishment. Transportation to penal colonies overseas and the building of new prisons offered alternative punishments and aimed to reform criminals.

I n 1868, after considerable parliamentary debate and increased pressure from campaigners, public execution was abolished. This 'civilising moment' silenced the crowd and the critics but also the voice of the condemned and those campaigning to end the death penalty altogether. Now performed behind prison walls, invisible to the public eye, executions became more clinical and bureaucratic.

TRANSPORTATION

Britain's expanding empire provided an alternative punishment to execution. The transportation of convicts to America from 1718 supplied the plantations with some of the labour required to exploit the riches of the land. Although the American War of Independence (1775–83) halted transportation, a new opportunity soon arose with the colonisation of Australia. Between 1788 and 1868, over 160,000 convicts arrived in Australia from England and other parts of the British Empire. Britain's first penal colony in Australia was established in Botany Bay in 1788 with the arrival of 548 male and 188 female convicts. Although sentences ranged from seven years to life, convicts rarely returned home and transportation was viewed as a 'life sentence'. It could, however, be alleviated by a 'ticket of leave' for good behaviour. This offered limited freedoms and the chance to take up paid employment, to get married and to own property in the colony.

For some, transportation offered a welcome reprieve from the death penalty. John Robinson, aged 41, was sentenced to transportation for life in 1832. Earlier that year, his offence of horse stealing had been removed from the capital offences statute by Sir Robert Peel's government. The following year, John Darby, aged 39, had a similarly lucky escape. He was transported for life for forging a bill of exchange in January 1833, but was spared the death penalty, as most crimes of forgery had been abolished as a capital offence just months before his conviction. In 1833, a total of 36 convict ships with nearly 7,000 convicts sailed to the penal colonies in Australia, making a journey that took over three months.

Many prisoners who were transported to Australia would never have travelled far before. Some of those who were convicted had never left their home town or neighbourhood until their arrest. A three-month sea voyage across the world and the idea that they might never return must have been almost unimaginable. Some convicts awaiting transportation presented

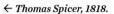

← *Thomas Spicer, 1818.*

Spicer was sentenced to death for counterfeiting banknotes; he was aged 17. His sentence was commuted to 14 years transportation to New South Wales. His sentence was further reduced and he was allowed to return to England in 1825.

← *J. Bretton, 1831.*

On one side, an image shows Bretton in chains staring after the departing ship that has taken him to Australia. On the other side, he asks his sister to 'Remember me When far Away'.

← *Lewis Lyon, 1831.*

Lyon's token refers to his sentence of 7 years transportation for the theft of cheese. After conviction he was taken to the prison hulk Retribution at Woolwich, until he sailed for Van Diemen's Land (Tasmania), along with 265 other convicts.

← *George Wright, 1826.*

Wright gifted this token to Ann Lee. He had been found guilty of stealing some silk and a handkerchief from a house in Spitalfields. Sentenced to death, he was instead transported for life to New South Wales aboard the Marquis of Huntley on 10 May 1826.

loved ones with coins engraved with messages of affection, often paying fellow prisoners who were skilled in metalworking to create the tokens. Known as 'leaden hearts', they reflected the convicts' fear of never returning home.

↑ The treadmill at the House of Correction, Brixton, 1821.
ENGRAVING BY JOHN SHURY, 1821.

PRISON REFORM

From the late 18th century, penal reformers, including John Howard, looked to the prison system as an alternative punishment to execution with the potential to reform criminals. Howard was an advocate for keeping prisoners in isolation, a practice that became known as the 'separate' system. Elizabeth Fry argued against this system in 1835 at the House of Lords 'Committee on the State of Gaols and Houses of Correction in England and Wales'. But, although the Committee took on a number of her suggestions, they were not won over by her dislike of the 'silent' and 'separate' systems. Newly built convict prisons, intended to reach the soul of the offender, adopted both methods to encourage reflection and a Christian life away

→ Prison ship at Deptford, 1826.
ENGRAVING BY GEORGE COOKE AFTER SAMUEL PROUT, 1826.

from crime. For example, Pentonville Prison, which opened in 1842 for the detention of those sentenced to imprisonment or awaiting transportation, operated on the 'separate' and 'silent' systems. Prisoners had their own cells and were forbidden to speak. Meanwhile, older prisons, such as Coldbath Fields, near Farringdon, where separate cells could not be introduced, banned prisoners from talking to each other.

The principle of hard labour ensured prisoners were productive and occupied. Brixton was the first prison to introduce a treadmill. Inmates spent up to ten hours climbing the revolving steps attached to millstones that ground flour for bread. Its perceived benefits in reforming criminals resulted in treadmills being installed in other prisons. These harsh regimes deprived prisoners of all human contact, resulting in many taking their own lives. Treadmills became notorious and featured in poems, such as Oscar Wilde's *The Ballad of Reading Gaol*, and novels, such as Charles Dickens's *Bleak House* and *A Christmas Carol*.

Prison ships or hulks were used from the 1770s, initially as a temporary measure to hold prisoners who could not be transported to the Americas because of the War of Independence there. However, these decommissioned warships were used for

'That many cartloads of our fellow-creatures are, once in 6 weeks, carried to slaughter is a dreadful consideration. And this is greatly heightened by reflection, that with proper care & proper regulation, much the greater part of these wretches might have been made into useful members of society.'

John Howard, philanthropist and prison reformer, 1777

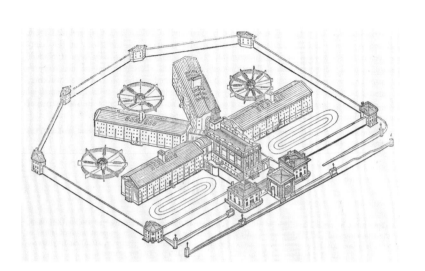

over half a century to house prisoners, including some of the most hardened offenders. The appalling verminous conditions led to many inmates succumbing to 'gaol fever' (typhus), cholera and typhoid. Henry Mayhew referred to the prison hulks anchored at Woolwich as the 'despair of all penal reformers'. Mayhew was a reforming journalist who had published a groundbreaking study of the poor of London in 1861. His follow-up work, *The Criminal Prisons of London and Scenes of Prison Life*, was written with John Binny and published the following year. This detailed investigation into London's prisons included oral testimony from prisoners and warders during visits to convict prisons, correctional prisons, women's prisons and the prison hulks at Woolwich.

THE ESTABLISHMENT OF THE METROPOLITAN POLICE FORCE

With the reduction of capital crimes, the state could no longer rely on the fear of execution for the prevention of crime. The necessity for a fresh approach to deterrence prompted the creation of a professional Metropolitan Police Force by the Home Secretary, Sir Robert Peel, in 1829.

Peel's visible force replaced the disparate local services that had previously protected London. The purpose of the initial 3,200 police officers was to prevent future crime and to instil the fear of detection in potential criminals. In 1842, a detective department was created to ensure that solving crime became more a matter of certainty than chance.

The prime duty of the new officers was surveillance. They were required to walk their neighbourhood beat at a regulation slow

'...the execution of a person is the act of the whole nation, and that being so, it should be done in public...'
Charles Newdegate, politician, 1868

pace, armed with a truncheon. A rattle, later replaced by a whistle, was also carried to attract attention when chasing criminals. Police officers walked the beat in top hats and blue swallow-tailed coats. The high collar concealed a leather band to prevent attacks from behind. The civilian-style uniform was intended to allay fears of a comparison between the police and the military. Despite these efforts, police officers, commonly called Peelers or Bobbies, after Sir Robert Peel, were initially unpopular with many working-class Londoners who feared a loss of their liberty.

CRITICISM OF PUBLIC EXECUTION

The effectiveness of public execution as a deterrent to crime had been debated since the late 18th century. The campaign to abolish the death sentence for at least some crimes gained strength in the early years of the 19th century. Particular attention was given to forgery, as many people felt that non-violent crimes deserved a lesser punishment. The case of the forger Henry Fauntleroy attracted particular sympathy and, although public concern in Fauntleroy's case failed to save him, it did influence the decision to abolish execution for most forms of forgery in 1832 and for all with the Forgery Act 1837. But even with crimes where execution was regarded as the correct punishment, there was sometimes unease at the public's reaction to the spectacle. In 1830, when William Sapwell was executed for the murder of a police officer, John Long, the *Atlas* newspaper reported:

> We regret to add, that the assembled multitude expressed their horror of the crime by adding anguish to the last hour of the criminal; another proof that the frequent sight of punishment hardens the heart. The punishment of the law was just and necessary; the simultaneous hiss of the mob, uncalled for, cruel and unchristian.

By the mid 19th century, concerns about the morality of the execution crowd peaked. Watching an execution was regarded as 'uncivilised' by the emerging middle class who feared it brutalised society. Public pain and death became morally unacceptable to squeamish Victorians. The novelists Charles Dickens and William Thackeray attended the execution of Swiss-born

↑ *Police Constable Vincent in uniform, c. early 1860s.* Note his high, stiff collar and the top hat that he holds in his hand. The uniform was updated in 1863 and the top hat was replaced with a helmet.

'*The horrors of the gibbet and of the crime which brought the wretched murderers to it faded in my mind before the atrocious bearing, looks and language of the assembled spectators.*'
Charles Dickens, author, 1849

↑ *Crowds gather for the execution of Maria and Frederick Manning at Horsemonger Lane Gaol, 1849.*
INK WASH DRAWING, 1849.

← *Explosion at the House of Detention, Clerkenwell, 13th December 1867.*

This is the explosion for which Michael Barrett was executed in 1868, the last person to be publicly executed in London. The image shows the level of destruction wrought on both the House of Detention and the surrounding tenements, where two children died.
ILLUSTRATED LONDON NEWS, 21 DECEMBER 1867

François Courvoisier in 1840. Nicknamed 'The Swiss Valet', he had been found guilty of the murder of his master, Lord William Russell, and his execution attracted huge crowds. Both authors wrote about their experience. Dickens focused on the execution scene, noting there was 'nothing but ribaldry, debauchery, levity, drunkenness and flaunting vice', while Thackeray reflected: 'I feel myself ashamed and degraded at the brutal curiosity which took me to that brutal sight.'

When Maria and Frederick Manning, the first married couple to be executed since 1700, were hanged on 13 November 1849, an 'immense assemblage' of people waited outside the gaol. The crowd laughed, joked, danced, drank, fought and picked pockets. Dickens was again among them and wrote a furious letter to *The Times* criticising the 'wickedness and levity' of the crowd, calling their behaviour 'inconceivably awful'. He described public execution as a 'moral evil' that should be rooted out, doubting that communities could prosper where such scenes of 'horror and demoralisation' could take place. Such concerns did not represent greater sympathy with the condemned but rather the desire to establish modern standards of conduct and control the urban masses.

The growing unease about the spectacle of public execution became more widespread. In 1850, a cartoon published in the satirical magazine *Punch*, entitled 'The Trial for Murder Mania', mocked the commercialisation of state executions and the public's obsession with crime and punishment.

Executions in public, before a crowd, were increasingly seen as inappropriate for a civilised society. The Royal Commission on Capital Punishment was set up in 1864 and sat for two years. It concluded that, although the death penalty should remain, public execution should end in Great Britain and Ireland.

THE LAST PUBLIC EXECUTION IN LONDON

The Irish republican Michael Barrett was the last person to be publicly executed in London. He was condemned for his role in the explosion at the Clerkenwell House of Detention, a failed

↑ *Broadside for François Courvoisier, known as 'The Swiss Valet', executed for murder, 1840.*

attempt by Irish Fenians (republicans) to rescue one of their leaders held in the prison. The dynamite blew a hole in the prison wall but also destroyed a number of tenement dwellings killing several residents, including two children. Barrett always protested his innocence and claimed to have been in Glasgow at the time but was condemned on a false statement by a fellow Irishman. Thousands travelled to Newgate on the Underground, the world's first underground railway network, to witness his death on 26 May 1868. London was modernising and the abolition of public execution three days later seemed an inevitable consequence of a changing society.

↑ *The last execution at Newgate, 1868.*
A graphic illustration of the crowds at Barrett's execution, with fights breaking out and and a ginger pop seller pulling his cart through the melee.
ENGRAVING, C.1868.

CONCLUSION

EXECUTIONS MOVE INSIDE

The Capital Punishment Amendment Act of 1868 relocated the theatre of death from the public arena to the privacy of prison grounds. With the exclusion of the crowd, executions became more standardised and sanitised, with all aspects tightly controlled by the state. However, public interest remained, now experienced and channelled through more formalised processes such as newspaper reports. Crowds still turned out on execution day to throng the prison gates, but in much more limited numbers and in a much more controlled manner.

Hailed as a triumph of advancement, the Act removed the alarming spectacle around the gallows, but also dampened support for the abolition of the death penalty, and this punishment remained a feature of the British legal system for a further 100 years. Between 1868 and 1961, 335 people were executed inside London's prisons. Executions ended completely at Horsemonger Lane in 1877. In 1902, the last execution took place at Newgate; from then, all men in London were executed at either Wandsworth Prison (south of the River Thames), or Pentonville Prison (north of the River Thames) and all women at Holloway Prison. The last woman to face the Holloway gallows was Ruth Ellis. Her execution in 1955 proved a catalyst in the debate on the abolition of the death penalty for murder in the UK and she was the last woman to be executed in Great Britain. Following a number of other controversial executions, the death penalty was suspended in England, Wales and Scotland in 1965, and abolished in 1969, but remained available in Northern Ireland until 1973. Treason remained punishable by death until the complete abolition of the death penalty under the Crime and Disorder Act of 1998.

'...if criminals were executed within the prison walls, and seen no more by the public after trial and sentence, it would strike terror and dismay to the wicked.'

Thomas Redin, prison governor, 1856

THE BLOODY CODE

In 1723, an Act was passed which greatly expanded the number of crimes for which an individual could be executed – the Black Act. Further crimes were added over the years, and this list of crimes became known as the 'Bloody Code'. They were repealed by Acts in 1823 and 1827 as part of Sir Robert Peel's reforms of British criminal law. The list below identifies the crimes covered by the Bloody Code. 153 offences are listed but, as certain offences cover multiple crimes, there are actually more than 200 different capital offences.

Treason ✝ Murder ✝ Robbery ✝ Burglary ✝ Theft ✝ Rape ✝ Burning a dwelling house ✝ Counterfeiting money ✝ Heresy ✝ Manslaughter ✝ Forcible marriage ✝ Buggery ✝ Refusing to take the Oath of Supremacy ✝ Witchcraft ✝ Piracy ✝ Robbing a church ✝ Robbing persons in dwelling houses ✝ Highway robbery ✝ Stealing a horse ✝ Wilfully burning barns with corn ✝ Maliciously maiming or disfiguring any person, ✝ Lying in wait to maim or disfigure any person ✝ Robbing a booth or tent ✝ Being an accessory to stealing a horse ✝ Being an accessory to murder ✝ Being an accessory to burning a dwelling house ✝ Being an accessory to robbing a dwelling house ✝ Being an accessory to highway robbery ✝ Egyptians remaining within the kingdom one month ✝ Counterfeiting the Great or Privy Seal ✝ Counterfeiting foreign coins ✝ Importing counterfeit foreign coins ✝ Taking away any maid, widow or wife ✝ Clipping, washing or filing coins ✝ Impairing, diminishing or scaling coins ✝ Robbing houses in the daytime of the value of 5 shillings ✝ Stealing from the person ✝ Embezzling arrears and victuals of soldiers ✝ Forgery ✝ Stabbing ✝ Concealing the birth of a bastard child, with evidence of murder ✝ Levying a fine in the name of another ✝ Shooting at a person ✝ Drawing the trigger of a gun at a person ✝ Malicious burning in the night stacks of corn or hay, barns, houses, buildings or kilns ✝ Killing or destroying horses, sheep or cattle in the night ✝ Master or mariner casting away, burning or destroying a ship ✝ Stealing cloth from the rack ✝ Possession of coining implements ✝ Removing coining implements from the Mint ✝ Milling counterfeit or diminished money, or washing blanks ✝ Blanching copper for sale ✝ Receiving or paying counterfeit money at less than denomination ✝ Piracy under commission of a foreign prince ✝ Assisting to break into a dwelling house, shop or warehouse and stealing over 5 shillings although no person therein ✝ Stealing over 5 shillings from a shop, warehouse, coach house or stable ✝ Being an accessory to receiving stolen goods ✝ Attempting the life of a Privy Counsellor in the execution of his office ✝ Master or mariner casting away, burning or destroying a ship to defraud the insurer ✝ Making holes in a ship in distress stealing the pump, or doing any other thing tending to loss or destruction ✝ Stealing over 40 shillings from a dwelling house ✝ Forging or uttering certain instruments to defraud the South Sea Company ✝ Rioters not dispersing after Proclamation ✝ Rioters demolishing churches, chapels or dissenting meeting houses ✝ Rioters demolishing houses, barns, stables or outhouses ✝ Returning from transportation ✝ Being armed with face blackened or otherwise disguised in any high road, open heath, common, or down ✝ Being armed with face blackened or otherwise disguised in any forest, chase, park, paddock or grounds where deer are usually kept ✝ Being armed with face blackened or otherwise disguised in any warrens or other places where hares or rabbits are usually kept ✝ Unlawfully hunting, wounding, killing, destroying or stealing deer ✝ Stealing rabbits or hares ✝ Robbing rabbit warrens ✝ Stealing or taking any fish out of any river or pond ✝ Hunting in His Majesty's forests or chases ✝ Breaking down the head or mound of a fish pond whereby fish shall be lost or destroyed ✝ Maliciously killing, maiming or wounding cattle ✝ Maliciously cutting down any trees planted in any avenue or growing in any garden, orchard or plantation ✝ Setting fire to a house, barn, outhouse, hovel, cock, mow, stack of corn, straw, hay or wood ✝ Wilfully and maliciously shooting any person in any dwelling house ✝ Wilfully and maliciously shooting any person in any other place ✝ Sending anonymous letters demanding money ✝ Sending letters demanding money signed with a fictitious name ✝ Forcibly rescuing any person being lawfully in the custody of any officer or other person for any such offence ✝ Procuring by gift or promise of money or other reward any of His Majesty's subjects to join him or them in any unlawful act ✝ Taking a reward for helping another to stolen goods ✝ Trading, corresponding with or assisting pirates ✝ Forging or uttering certain instruments to defraud the London or Royal Exchange Assurance ✝ Forging or uttering power to transfer stock of company established by Act of Parliament, or to receive dividends, false impersonating for defrauding companies ✝ Forging or uttering instruments respecting money in office of Accountant General, East India or South Sea bonds ✝ Bankrupts not surrendering ✝ Bankrupts concealing or embezzling their effects ✝ Destroying any fence, lock or sluice ✝ Making a false entry in a marriage register ✝ Sending threatening letters ✝ Destroying banks at Bedford Level ✝ Enlisting in the Foreign Service without consent of His Majesty ✝ Accepting a Commission from the King of France without leave ✝ Engaging others to go beyond sea with intent to be enlisted in the Foreign Service ✝ Gilding silver coins to look like gold, or copper to look like silver ✝ Knowingly uttering counterfeit money (third offence) ✝ Setting fire to coal mines ✝ Destroying turnpikes ✝ Demolishing locks of a navigable river ✝ Cutting down sea banks or banks of a river ✝ Cutting hop binds ✝ Sending anonymous letters threatening to murder, burn houses or barns ✝ Assisting the enemy at sea ✝ Plundering goods from a wreck ✝ Obstructing persons endeavouring to save their lives from shipwreck ✝ Putting out false lights to bring a vessel into danger ✝ Stealing over 40 shillings from a ship in a navigable river or creek ✝ Stealing sheep or other cattle ✝ Stealing linen from a bleaching ground ✝ Embezzlement by servants of a bank ✝ Embezzlement by servants of the South Sea Company ✝ Forging or uttering deed, will, bond, bill of exchange, premium note, indorsement of premium note, receipt for money or good with intent to defraud any person ✝

Forging a Mediterranean pass ✝ Forging acceptance of bill, accountable receipt etc. to defraud a person ✝ Forging banknote or bill, dividend warrant, bond of Bank of England indorsement ✝ Forging lottery tickets ✝ Being disguised within the Mint ✝ Injuring of Westminster Bridge and other bridges ✝ Harbouring offenders against the Revenue Act, when returned from transportation ✝ Attempting to seduce soldiers from their allegiance ✝ Administering unlawful oaths ✝ Seditious societies (writing or speaking against the monarch or their government) ✝ Counterfeiting copper coins ✝ Uttering counterfeit foreign money (third offence) ✝ Cutting or stabbing with intent to murder, rob, maim or do grievous bodily harm ✝ Administering poison with intent to murder ✝ Administering a draught to cause abortion for a woman quick with child ✝ Rioters demolishing mills or works thereto belonging ✝ Rioters demolishing buildings and engines used in trade or manufactory, or in which goods are warehoused ✝ Burning or destroying arsenals, magazines, dockyards or military stores ✝ Setting fire to ships ✝ Setting fire to a house, barn, hop oast, malt house, stable, coach house, outhouse, mill or shop in possession of an offender or other person with intent to defraud or injure ✝ Setting fire to buildings or engines ✝ Breaking into certain buildings with intent to steal out or destroy linens, yarn in looms, tools or implements ✝ Cutting linen laid to bleach ✝ Breaking into a house, shop with intent to destroy goods or tools, in woollen, silk, linen or cotton manufactures ✝ Cutting or destroying wool, silk, linen or cotton ✝ Breaking into a house or shop with intent to destroy goods or tools in stocking manufactory ✝ Burning a ship keel or other vessel ✝ Breaking into manufactories with intent to steal cloth ✝ Impersonating a pensioner of Greenwich Hospital ✝ Forgery or uttering instruments for transfer of stock ✝ Making or having in possession certain implements, paper etc. for forging banknotes ✝ Making or having in possession engravings to appear like banknotes ✝ Forging or uttering acceptance or accountable receipt to defraud a corporation ✝ Forging or uttering seamen's tickets for wages ✝ Possession of forged notes ✝ Forging, offering, disposing of or putting away a will, bond, bill, note, indorsement, acceptance, receipt or other security, warrant or order, banknotes, dividend warrants to defraud a person or corporation.

INDEX

ACKNOWLEDGEMENTS

The authors would like to thank all of the Executions exhibition team at the Museum of London, and in particular Rita Rooney and Nikki Braunton for their work on this book, and John Chase and Richard Stroud for the photography. Also, our thanks go to the prisoners and staff of HMP Pentonville, in particular Alan, Ali, Daniel, Harry, Michael, Richard, Tracy, José and Helena; our content contributors and advisors, in particular The King's Army of the English Civil War Society, Paul Bridges, Amnesty International, Scott Kelly, the Society of William Wallace; our editors at Philip Wilson Publishers, Clare Martelli and Natasha Collin; copy-editor, Vic Tebbs; and designer, Ocky Murray.

PICTURE CREDITS